The Ultimate ROTC Guidebook

David Atkinson

SB

Savas Beatie
New York and California

© 2012 by David Atkinson

All rights reserved. No part of this publication may be reproduced, stored in a retrieval system, or transmitted, in any form or by any means, electronic, mechanical, photocopying, recording, or otherwise, without the prior written permission of the publisher.

Cataloging-in-Publication Data is available from the Library of Congress.

ISBN-13: 978-1-61121-096-5

05 04 03 02 01 5 4 3 2 1
First Savas Beatie edition, first printing

SB

Published by
Savas Beatie LLC
521 Fifth Avenue, Suite 1700
New York, NY 10175

Editorial Offices:

Savas Beatie LLC
P.O. Box 4527
El Dorado Hills, CA 95762
916-941-6896
sales@savasbeatie.com

Savas Beatie titles are available at special discounts for bulk purchases in the United States by corporations, institutions, and other organizations. For more details, please contact Special Sales, P.O. Box 4527, El Dorado Hills, CA 95762, or you may e-mail us at sales@savasbeatie.com, or visit our website at www.savasbeatie.com for additional information.

Proudly published, printed, and warehoused in the United States of America.

Dedication

This book is dedicated to my Truman State University cadre, the University of Central Missouri ROTC program, fellow cadets, Dr. C, Ms. Presley, family, and friends. Without their support this document may very well have remained on my laptop. I appreciate every bit of help and encouragement I received. Lastly, I want to dedicate this to every cadet or future cadet reading this text for their commitment to serving this country.

Contents

Contents, Continued

All photographs courtesy of the University of Central Missouri
ROTC Department.
Front cover, left: author 2LT David Atkinson, right: 2LT Jeff Bohlman

Preface

You may not understand all the references in this Preface right now, but it will give you a feel for how I came to be in a position to write this book at all, and why I thought it was a good idea to do so. Maybe it would be a good idea for you to come back after you finish the book and read the Preface again! For now, just dive in.

When I first started college I had no desire to join ROTC. In high school I had met with recruiters from every branch of the military, including the Guard and Reserves, and when I decided on my university I spoke with a representative of its ROTC department. But afterward I was still unsure of what to expect from the program; was not too keen on having to wear a military uniform, for fear it would make me look like an outsider on campus; and did not want to commit myself to something before experiencing what else student life had to offer. I decided instead that I wanted to have a "college" experience.

But during my freshman year I was somehow enrolled in Military Science 100. Many students take it as an alternative to Health and Wellness; however, due to my major I would have to take Health and Wellness anyway. I did not know a single person in the class. Nonetheless I decided to stay in MS100. I stayed because it was easy—and enjoyable: it offered a little unconventional academic excitement. It was the only class on campus that let you go paintballing for lab and learn to start a fire and catch fish for survival. You could also feel a connection to something larger—in this case, the Army—without actually being a part of it. Even so, I did not join any extracurricular ROTC activities, such as Ranger Challenge or Color Guard.

Yet I ended up enjoying it so much that by the end of my freshman year I decided I wanted to contract as a cadet. I still, however, did not know a single person in the program, and was not really sure what it meant to be a cadet. I just thought I would enjoy the lifestyle, there were good scholarships, and I could serve my country. So over the summer I searched for any books I could find relating to ROTC. I may have found two, but neither explained how to be a successful cadet. Considering all the confusion and questions I had, I knew I couldn't be the only future cadet in the nation who didn't really know what he was getting himself into. Sure, the cadre would help answer questions; but, like most other cadets, I didn't even know what to ask, because I didn't know what I didn't know.

To join ROTC you must provide some proof that you have leadership potential; this usually amounts to listing any position you have held in an organization, on a sports team, etc. You must meet certain grade point average requirements. You must meet certain physical fitness requirements. You must go through a thorough physical examination by a doctor. To me it seemed as if the process of getting approval for a scholarship was never-ending. Fortunately, that was not the case. I raised my hand to take the oath on September 5th, 2007.

Right away I jumped whole-heartedly into the cadet culture. I bought an Army camouflage backpack, got chills the first time I put on the uniform, and began reading all the non-fiction military books I could get my hands on. I also tried to focus on raising my fitness test score by running hard, lifting hard, and doing countless pushups and situps. I was a natural runner, but the pushups and situps took some effort—doing fifty in two minutes was tough, doing sixty was almost asking too much.

A few weeks into the semester I was asked to go to a Ranger Challenge workout in the morning to see if I liked it. Part of me wanted to say no, because it meant waking up even earlier; but I went anyway. The first time I went, however, turned out to be the day they did the Army Physical Fitness Test so they could gauge where they stood. I collapsed after 66 pushups. I was amazed to watch the members of the A-team do 80, 90, or even a hundred with apparent ease. My competitive juices began flowing, and I decided this was something I wanted to do.

Through Ranger Challenge I made many friends, had many great experiences, and learned tons about the Army. About a month later, my class was told about an Air Assault slot that had opened up. I was at the top of our class' Order of Merit List, and therefore had first dibs. You might never actually use the knowledge from the school, but that was unimportant to me and most others at the time; the cool thing was that Air Assault school bestowed a badge upon completion, and I just wanted that badge to wear on my uniform, like so many of the cadre and upperclassmen. However, a week or two later information came out about a new program called Cultural Understanding and Language Proficiency (CULP). Information about it was scarce because it was so new, but it was clear that the cadets selected would get to travel to another country to do military training. Getting in wasn't guaranteed, like for Air Assault school, because slots were limited and there was an application process; but I decided to take my chances for the opportunity to travel abroad for free. My friend went to Air Assault instead and earned the badge; if I didn't get selected for CULP, I would be kicking myself for the next year. That semester I also joined Color Guard.

In the spring I decided to start a military-focused organization to enhance tactics and learn skills based on books I was reading about special operations. Nowadays it seems laughable, and it is easier to see that the cadre doubted it would take off or that anyone would want to show up and dedicate even more time to Army training. Our unofficial organization began with six members, including myself. We had no firm idea of what we wanted to do, and a couple of times our meetings ended up with us just playing Risk. That semester I was the only sophomore asked to lead a weekly PT session in the afternoon. Then, later that semester, I learned that I was one of 15 cadets from the nation selected to travel to Slovakia for three weeks as part of CULP! During this semester I also competed in the Ranger Challenge Buddy Team competition. My partner and I finished first overall in a couple of events, but the grenade course brought us down. We finished 3rd out of, I believe, 76 teams representing at least 12 different states.

CULP was a blast. The best part was that it was free and I made friends with everyone there. We stayed in incredible hotels, went mountain biking, hiked to the peak of a mountain, went on a riverboat cruise, went to a huge water park, and saw dozens of castles. We were also given the freedom to roam around the cities at night with little supervision, and it was refreshing to be treated as adults. For one week we trained with Slovakian cadets at their version of West Point. We had a great time, gained a much greater cultural perception, and made good friends with the Slovaks. I also spoke to the other U.S. cadets and the lieutenant colonel in charge of us about the club I had started with my friends, and began combing through information about other university programs, identifying what I believed were their best characteristics.

When I returned to school I implemented several changes to the club organization. We got it chartered as an official school organization, created a constitution, and revamped the entire training schedule. With this, we garnered more support from the cadre, and had 12 cadets join—roughly a fifth of the contracted cadets at the time. This was enough to form a squad, which was all we needed to run a STX lane. The organization has changed little since then.

I did Ranger Challenge again that fall. This time I made the A-team. We trained hard and had a great time, but finished a frustrating 3rd at competition due to poor throwing on the grenade assault course. I also started to assume more leadership roles because it was my junior year. Everyone in my class rotated through various positions. I was made the Platoon Leader for our fall FTX, and PL again for the spring JFTX. We also had to lead PT sessions and STX lanes in preparation for LDAC. (Please excuse the many acronyms. As I mentioned at the beginning, they will all make sense later in the book.) I tried to break STX lanes down into a science by dissecting every smallest phase of each type of mission. I transformed these breakdowns into diagrams and smart sheets (which can be found in this book's appendix). In the spring we also conducted the German Armed Forces Badge for Military Proficiency, a series of events that includes swimming, jumping, sprinting, running, shooting a pistol, and finally an 18.6-mile ruck march. I earned a gold badge—along with huge blisters on my feet.

At LDAC that summer I earned an overall E rating and held positions as company 1SG, patrol leader, squad leader, and recorder for most STX missions. I also earned the RECONDO badge for scoring well on the APFT and passing various tests on the first try, such as the obstacle course and first aid. Immediately after LDAC I flew to Europe (for free again!) to do Cadet Troop Leader Training in Germany for four weeks.

Upon returning to the states I learned I had been selected by the Professor of Military Science to be the cadet battalion commander. I was also a Ranger Challenge co-captain. Our team finished 3rd again—as before, it was those darn grenades. . . . In the spring I became the cadet S-3, or operations officer. The job involved planning and coordinating all training, with the help of the cadre. I also started taking Arabic, and through an Army Critical Language Program I was able to make extra money just for passing the class.

When I joined ROTC I had been given a 3.5 year contract, so I was able to spend an extra semester at college. In my final semester I learned I had placed within the top 10% of cadets in the nation, 80th overall. I chose to go on active duty, and chose to be in the Medical Service Corps. Later in the semester I learned I would be assigned to the 82nd Airborne Division at Fort Bragg, NC.

In January 2011 I began Basic Officer Leadership Course (BOLC). Throughout its two and a half months I had a great time making many good friends. Because we were medically oriented, we trained in San Antonio, TX, which is where most Army medical training takes place. Often after class and every weekend we would drive five miles to the river walk and have fun swapping stories about the week. The Army Medical Department (AMEDD) is a different breed from the rest of the Army. It has a different promotion system, and the branch is made up of a much greater variety of soldiers. There were people from all walks of medical life, in all stages of their life cycles, with vastly different amounts of military experience. For example, we had a dental specialist who joined the Army in his fifties and was made a lieutenant colonel, despite being associated with the military for less time than nearly everyone else. Alongside someone so brand-new were former Special Forces NCOs who had decided to become physician assistants. In the end I was one of four nominated by our platoon advisor for the top leadership award for our class. My platoon, including myself, ended up giving the majority of our votes to one of the physician assistants I mentioned to represent us. I was glad just to be nominated in the same category as the other three.

After BOLC I attended Airborne School, which is known for being tediously long. (Some say it's where they cram five days of training into three weeks.) I learned how to exit an aircraft, how to fall, and how to hit the ground without getting injured. During the final week we jumped from a plane five times in order to earn the Airborne badge.

In May I moved to Fort Bragg, and am now a medical platoon leader and the medical officer for the squadron. Active duty life is very different from cadet life. The hours are long, the tasks are many, and the learning curve is steep. However, I fully believe that my ROTC program prepared me well to deal with the situations I face. I hope that this book will help you be successful in your ROTC experience, so that you too can achieve a feeling of satisfaction and become an effective and successful Army officer. Airborne!

David Atkinson
2LT, MS
September 2011

Acknowledgements

In the writing of this book I had help from two cadets, Christopher Moe and Andrew Tipping, and the assistance of Lieutenant Colonel Douglas Reinsch. They offered great advice. Moe reviewed the patrolling and STX sections. Tipping did an excellent job reviewing the entire document, and offered loads of feedback. LTC R reviewed the section on what Truman does well. I want to thank all of them for their input. In addition, I know ROTC is an ever-evolving entity and any questions, comments, updates, or suggestions for this text are whole-heartedly welcome to ensure this book remains the best product available.

Introduction

Upon entering the Army as an active-duty officer, you will be confronted with a vast body of resources on how to perform your duties and meet applicable standards. Officers can find information in field manuals, Department of the Army (DA) pamphlets, and Army Training and Education Program publications (ARTEPs), as well as non-governmental books. In addition, various conferences around the globe serve as venues for exchanging and coordinating ideas, theories, and plans, the proceedings of which are then published. However, little material exists that is specifically designed for cadets currently in Reserve Officer Training Corps (ROTC) programs or people who want to know about such programs. Military Science (MS) courses use textbooks, but they primarily provide a general familiarization with the Army and what life will be like as an officer, whereas University handbooks tend to be about the history, regulations, and formalities associated with cadet status. Somehow, no one has developed a reference specifically designed to prepare young people for life as a cadet, then to help those cadets succeed in general, and particularly to help individuals improve their university battalions and score higher on the national Order of Merit List (OML).

That's where this reference guide comes in. It provides thorough coverage of how you can perform better in nearly every aspect of cadet life. It also includes suggestions on how to improve your battalion. Part One, the first portion of the book, covers improving yourself, and is fairly self-explanatory. However, just to ensure that everyone begins on the same page before delving into the specifics, here is a brief rundown on what each topic entails.

As a cadet, much will be expected of you. You must meet uniform standards, grooming standards, and time standards. Information about those aspects is typically found in each university's own cadet handbook. But you will also need to know how to do well during land navigation, perform strongly on the Army Physical Fitness Test (APFT), lead a squad through Situational Training Exercise (STX) lanes, and much more—at the highest level possible. This guide will give you an edge by supplying you, in an organized manner, with various tips that you can easily implement with a little practice.

Why do you need to perform so well? Because it will affect your standing on the national OML, and that may have a great impact on your life. The OML is broken down into various categories, with each section worth a designated number of points. Simply put, the more points you can garner, the more choices you will have; and to gain the most points overall, you must score the maximum according to the criteria for each category. You will be rated in camp, on land navigation, for involvement in intramural sports, and on many other aspects of your performance. At the beginning of your last year of ROTC, those points will be combined and entered into a national database that will rank every cadet in the nation, from the person with the most points to the person with the fewest. Every fraction of a point will matter, because the resultant ranking will determine whether you can serve on active duty rather than in the Reserves or Guard, and which job you will get. In essence, it will determine a lot about the next chunk of your life after college.

That's one reason this guide is essential reading for anyone hoping to perform to the best of his or her abilities in ROTC. Another, even more important, reason is that you should want to do well in order to be better prepared to serve your country, and the men and women whom you will lead as an officer.

Breakdown of Accessions Points

- The top five members of their platoon at Leader Development and Assessment Course (LDAC) receive one bonus point
- Earning the reconnaissance commando (RECONDO) ribbon at LDAC is worth half a bonus point

Academics (40% of total)

(40.0) Cumulative grade point average (GPA) of all academic subjects (includes ROTC GPA) (spring semester, most current)

Leadership (45% of total)

LDAC

(6.75)—LDAC Performance: Excellent (E)/ Satisfactory (S)/Needs improvement (N)
—Leadership positions
—Leadership attributes/skills/actions

(11.25)—LDAC Platoon Tactics Officer (TAC) Evaluation (E/S/N)

(4.50)—LDAC Land Navigation (1st score)

Professor of Military Science (PMS) Observations

(6.75)—PMS MS III Comprehensive Evaluation Report (CER) OML

(4.50)—PMS Accessions OML

(4.50)—PMS Accessions Potential Comments

(4.50)—Cadet Training/Extracurricular Activities

Examples: Color guard, drill team, ranger challenge, ROTC recruiter, debate team, elected official of an organization, peer educator/tutor, part-time job, U.S. Army Reserve/ National Guard/Simultaneous Membership Program (USAR/NG/SMP), community service, student government member, band member, leader (president/captain) of an extracurricular activity/club, dormitory resident advisor, full-time job, etc.

(2.25)—Language/Cultural Awareness

Examples: Major in a critical language, major in a non-critical language, pass a critical language course, pass a non-critical language course, complete Rosetta Stone for a critical language, complete Rosetta Stone for a non-critical language, study abroad in a non-English foreign country, etc.

Physical (15% of total)

APFT

(1.69)—Campus (MS III, fall semester)
(2.36)—Campus (MS III, spring semester)
(9.45)—LDAC (1st score)

Athletics

(1.50)—Varsity, intramural, or community team
NOTE: A perfect score would be 101.5 points.

Part Two of this manual is about improving your school's battalion. Doing so is beneficial not just to your institution but to the nation. Plus, it provides a way for you to excel as a cadet now, and to raise the bar for future officers. Some of the tips and ideas offered may already have been implemented in your ROTC program or battalion. If so, great; if not, your battalion should consider implementing these practices, or modified versions of them.

As a cadet, you can use all the ideas that follow to help you rise above and beyond the average. As a future leader, you should never settle for anything below the standard, and you are not doing your country proper service unless you strive to exceed the standard.

This document's layout resembles the LDAC timeline. First it discusses the importance of a strong grade point average and gives tips on how to achieve good grades. Next comes a discussion of physical fitness and nutrition, because without this solid base you will not be able to perform other military activities to a high standard. Following that is information on garrison leadership; you'll see a lot of that. Then it discusses land navigation, the field leadership reaction course (FLRC), situational training exercises (STX), and patrolling tips and examples. The last sections in the first part of this handbook contain general tips for performing well as a college student/cadet and at LDAC, and some thoughts on leadership philosophies derived from the experience of Army officers from junior ranks through field grade.

In the appendices at the back there is additional information, including a list of acronyms, abbreviations, and specialized terms and their meanings. Do not hesitate to look up words or terms you are unfamiliar with.

In order for this guide to be most advantageous for you, you should ask your 400s (fourth-year students, i.e., seniors) and cadre (training personnel) any questions you have about its contents. This handbook is intended not only to guide you toward optimal performance, but to stir critical, innovative thinking as well.

Commissioning Ceremony

Part One:

How To Improve Yourself

Chapter 1

Education

Grades are incredibly important. They comprise 40% of the total points on the national Order of Merit List (OML). Furthermore, the more you learn, the more knowledgeable you will be, which will make you a more capable, more respected officer.

The following tips will make you a more effective learner and better student, and earn you a higher grade point average (GPA) and OML ranking.

Attend All Classes

Be present for class whenever you can. This will help you grasp some concepts that are simply too difficult to understand through textbooks alone. Plus, many courses check attendance.

While in class, actively participate. Ask questions and answer questions posed by the professor and your classmates. If you are uncomfortable asking your questions in front of the class, jot them down on a piece of paper, catch your professor after class, and ask them then. By actively engaging you are more likely to pay attention, and therefore to understand what's going on. Missing classes will prevent you from doing the best you can.

Establish Regular Study Habits

Set aside a time of day when you simply sit down and power through homework. Make sure there are no distractions (TV, music, loud roommates, or the like) and that you are not studying during a time of day when you will be apt to fall asleep. For many people, the best place to study is an individual desk at the campus library, away from other students. The less distracted you are, the more quickly you will finish studying, and the sooner you can get back to doing whatever else you want to do.

Also, try to study each subject for at least ten minutes a day. This keeps the material fresh, and may raise questions that you did not think of during class.

Ask for Help

Don't be afraid to talk with classmates, meet with tutors or teaching assistants, or visit the professor during office hours. Sometimes a fifteen-minute, one-on-one discussion is all it takes to clarify a concept so that the rest of the material makes sense, and the rest of your semester will go much more smoothly. Professors and tutors get paid to answer your questions, so use them.

Use a Planner

Often in college you will simply have too much going on to know what you should be doing at all times. Use a planner to write down test dates, the times of meetings, when homework is due, and even lists of more minor tasks, such as "schedule an appointment with academic advisor." A planner will help you stay on top of things. Don't be the kid who always has to be reminded what to do.

Learn to Say No

In college there are lots of things that can distract you from academics and Reserve Officer Training Corps (ROTC): friends asking you to hang out, movies being shown on campus, and organizations that soak up valuable time through meetings and events. Sometimes you need to be able to just say "No" so that you can focus on your top priorities first.

Drawing up your to-do list should be at the top of your to-do list. Doing so will give you more time to focus on the tasks that need to be accomplished, and will ease the stress of trying to fit everything into a small time frame. Consider writing a time-use journal covering a few days to see where you actually spend your time.

You will not be able to do everything you want to, but you can do everything that you need to—if you prioritize.

Don't Wait Until the Last Second

When working on homework, it's very important to leave wiggle room; something may come up. Some procrastination is unavoidable for almost everyone, but turning in late assignments is not. Finish a full draft of your work at least a day early so there's plenty of time to revise and complete it in a thorough manner.

Sometimes you'll get lucky when doing tasks at the last minute, but it's more likely to leave you falling behind and feeling stressed. You want to be an officer in the most powerful Army in the world; that requires you to be responsible and disciplined.

Practice Good Note Taking

Professors will often state something more than once or with obvious emphasis if it is something you should know for an upcoming quiz or exam. Pay attention for these clues and write the emphasized information down.

Write down complete thoughts. Too often students jot something down, thinking they will know what it refers to when they reread it, only to be confused when they try to study their own notes later on.

Get to Know Your Professors

Meet with your professors during their office hours to discuss your class; sit in the front row so they recognize your face; and work hard on assignments. The more comfortable you are in class and around your professor, the better off you'll be.

Study any old tests that professors may offer as practice material for upcoming tests, and always use any study guides they may make available. Knowing what kinds of questions professors like to ask will help you choose effective study methods that focus on the most important material.

Chapter 2

Physical Fitness

There are a number of myths about training for the Army Physical Fitness Test (APFT); almost every cadet will have tips on what will make you run faster, do more push-ups, and complete more sit-ups. The guidance provided here is based on research literature. (A list of standard APFT preparation exercises can be found in Appendix D.)

Physical fitness is imperative, and understanding how your body works and the specific benefits of maintaining an exercise regimen will reinforce that concept. To understand why some workouts work and others do not, you must know what physiological changes are taking place within your body as you exercise, so parts of this section constitute a crash course on exercise physiology.

Principles of Exercise

- *Balance*—Ensure that you are not over-working some muscle groups and under-working others. For example, the Army tends to neglect lower back exercises. Similarly, most males who go to the gym stress lifting for the chest and arms, but do not do enough lifting with their legs. Following a balanced workout plan is important to overall fitness.

- *Specificity*—Train for what you will be doing. When considering an exercise, ask yourself: "What will this movement help me improve?" If the answer is that it does not relate to any real-life usage, replace it.
- *Overload*—This is the concept of pushing your muscles to handle a little more intense workout than they are used to in order to improve. This is why you add weight at the gym or run speed intervals at the track: to become stronger and faster, respectively.
- *Progression*—Fitness takes time. To lift too heavy or run too fast too soon invites injury and will "de-motivate" you. The trick is to gradually improve your fitness, remaining aware of what you are and are not capable of at the moment, and realizing that, with time and effort, you can eventually improve.
- *Variety*—This is what helps keep you motivated and coming back for more. In addition, it keeps your body "on its toes," with your muscles constantly breaking down so as to build up stronger, thereby making them more capable of doing a wider range of movements effectively. Aim to do an extensive array of exercises that will keep your workouts fresh.
- *Regularity*—In order to actually see improvement, you have to continue exercising. Fitness is not something that will happen on its own. Most people can safely lift two to four times a week, and do cardio workouts four to six times a week.
- *Recovery*—During rest and recovery your body will rebuild into a stronger unit. This is most relevant in lifting; however, you should also position easy days of running between hard days.

Components of Health Fitness

- *Muscular Strength*—This is the force your muscles can produce during a single contraction. The best way to improve it is through resistance training.

- *Muscular Endurance*—This is the number of repetitions your muscles can do over a certain period. This is mostly what the two minutes of push-ups and sit-ups test for during the APFT. You improve it through high-repetition training.
- *Cardiovascular Fitness*—This is the ability of your heart to pump blood through your circulatory system to supply your body tissues with oxygen. Improve this through cardio workouts, such as running.
- *Body Composition*—This is the ratio of fat-free mass (FFM) (bones, minerals, blood, etc.) in your body to your fat mass (FM). To increase your FFM and decrease your FM, simply work out more and watch your diet.
- *Flexibility*—This is the range of movement your various joints can manage. To improve it, do static stretching *after* your workouts, when your muscles and other body tissues are warm and more elastic.

FITT Planning

When creating a workout program, be sure to consider all of the FITT principles, explained below:

- *Frequency*—How often will you work out that particular muscle group or body system? The discussion of "Regularity" above provided some general recommendations; adjust these based on your individual fitness level.
- *Intensity*—How hard will you work out? See the discussion above about letting your body recover; how often and how much you do so can be based on such things as your heart rate and your rating of perceived exertion, explained below.
- *Time*—This is the duration of the exercise: how long it lasts. As a general guideline, non-athletes needn't work out for more than an hour at a time. Consider this when deciding how far you should run, for example.
- *Type*—What exercises will you be doing? Why will you be doing them? Make sure they meet the standards of the "Specificity" principle discussed above.

Rating of Perceived Exertion (RPE) Scale

The RPE scale works by asking someone for a perception of how hard he or she is working out, on a scale from 6 to 20. Adding a zero to the end of that number should correlate to heart rate. Example: A 7 should correspond to about 70 beats per minute.

6
7 very, very light exertion
8
9 very light exertion
10
11 fairly light exertion
12
13 somewhat hard exertion
14
15 hard exertion
16
17 very hard exertion
18
19 very, very hard exertion
20

Classification of Physical Activity Intensity			
Intensity	%HRmax	RPE	%1RM
Very Light	<50	<10	<30
Light	60-63	10-11	30-49
Moderate	64-76	12-13	50-69
Hard (vigorous)	77-93	14-16	70-84
Very Hard	>94	17-19	>85
Maximal	100	20	100
HRmax = heart rate max. IRM = the most weight you can move in one repetition.			

What Happens When You Work Out

As you sit reading this, you are burning 5 Kcal (equal to the 5 calories you may see listed on the nutrition label of food) with each breath you take. When you work out, your breathing becomes more labored, and in the process you burn more calories. This increase in breathing is largely driven by your body's need to rid itself of carbon dioxide.

As you increase your workload, a few things happen within your body. Your heart rate (HR) continues to rise until it reaches its maximum (as a rule of thumb, max HR = 220 minus your age) or you quit working out. Your heart's stroke volume (the amount of blood your heart can pump per beat) increases up to the point where it is filled to its max (roughly at 60% of your max workout ability). Also, your body shifts from burning mostly fat (as it does at rest) to burning mostly carbohydrates.

Advantages of Aerobic and Anaerobic Exercise

Your body creates energy two different ways during aerobic ("with oxygen") and anaerobic ("without oxygen") exercise. During short bursts of activity your body almost exclusively uses chemical reactions to produce energy. However, during extended exertion, such as when running, your body uses oxygen as it creates energy. Anaerobic training prepares your body for activities such as lifting and sprinting, which more closely relate to strength. Aerobic activities are geared toward building endurance, muscular as well as cardiorespiratory.

With regular exercise and with aerobic activities in particular, several aspects of health and fitness conditioning begin to change. It's important to know why you want these changes to occur:

- *Stroke volume*—Being able to pump out more blood per beat means that you will be able to deliver oxygen and nutrients more efficiently to your body tissues, including your muscles.
- *VO2 max*—This is the maximum rate at which your body is able to consume oxygen. To get an accurate reading on what your

VO2 max currently is, you'd need to take a graded exercise test (GXT); but unless you plan on being an elite endurance athlete, that's unnecessary. All you need to know is that performing aerobic exercise will increase your VO2 max, and this one statistic is often cited as the best indicator of overall health by fitness professionals. People with a high VO2 max live longer, and a higher VO2 max will allow you to exercise at a higher intensity longer.

- *Mitochondria and mitochondrial enzymes*—These work at the cellular level to help provide your body with energy. If you are deficient in mitochondria, you feel fatigued more quickly. Likewise, the more you have, the longer you are able to maintain a high intensity. Think of mitochondria as little factories, and the enzymes as machinery in the factories.
- *Heart rate*—Working out makes your heart stronger, which means its resting rate—the beats per minute that it pumps—will decrease. A lower resting heart rate means your heart does not have to work as hard to get blood pumped throughout your body.
- *High Density Lipoprotein (HDL) cholesterol*—This is commonly referred to as "good cholesterol." Unlike Low Density Lipoprotein (LDL) cholesterol, which clogs your blood vessels, HDL cleans them out.
- *Glycogen storage*—Glycogen is a form of carbohydrates, which are your body's preferred energy source. Better glycogen storage allows you to exercise for longer, as your body is able to store and use it more efficiently.

Now for the specifics:

- *Stroke volume*—Sedentary people have stroke volumes at rest of about 60ml, whereas those of athletes often measure greater than 100ml. Training can increase the maximal stroke volume from 100 to 120 ml/beat to 180 to 200 ml/beat. However, when you stop training there is a rapid decrease (about 10 to 14% in 12 days).

- *Cardiac output*—This is the beats per minute times stroke volume (bpm x sv). Maximal cardiac output is only about 20 L/min in untrained individuals, whereas athletes may have maximal outputs ranging between 30 and 40 L/min.
- *VO2 max*—You can reasonably expect a 10 to 20% increase when starting an aerobic exercise program. (Don't worry too much about these specific numbers unless you are truly interested, in which case you should consider contacting an exercise physiologist to address your questions.) The average VO2 max scores for college-aged males are 44 to 51 ml/kg/min; for females 35 to 43 ml/kg/min. So, for example, with exercise you could expect to increase from 40 ml/kg/min (below average) to 48 ml/kg/min (upper level of average). The good news is that your VO2 max improves fairly rapidly, and it's easier to maintain it than it is to build it. So, after several weeks of hard training that will raise it, you can actually maintain it for several weeks even if you decrease your intensity by as much as 66%. The bad news is that you cannot just stop working out: after only 21 days of rest, your VO2 max will decrease by about 7%.
- *Mitochondria*—As with your VO2 max, the level of mitochondria in your muscles will decrease in just a matter of weeks.
- *Heart Rate*—With increased exercise, the resting heart rate can drop 1 to 2 beats per minute every 1 to 2 weeks for the first 10 to 20 weeks of an exercise program.
- *Blood volume*—With aerobic exercise, blood volume increases 20 to 25%.
- *Energy source*—With aerobic exercise, the body increases its capacity to use fat as an energy source at high workloads, rather than just using carbohydrates.
- *HDL*—Your HDL levels will rise with exercise, which can have a significant effect on your health. In fact, HDL levels are the only health factor that tends to compensate for health risks, such as smoking, obesity, high total cholesterol levels, and high blood pressure.

Musculoskeletal Fitness

Some benefits are most closely related to aerobic exercise (such as running, swimming, and cycling), whereas other factors of physiological health may improve with weight-bearing activities. The latter include stronger, thicker bones, stronger tendons and ligaments, and increased cartilage thickness; plus, of course, increased muscle strength.

What changes can you reasonably expect, and why? To begin with, don't get carried away with your ability to make massive gains in

Summary of Changes in Cardiorespiratory Parameters with Endurance Training			
Cardiovascular parameter	**Resting**	**Submax exercise**	**Max exercise**
Oxygen Consumption	no change	no change	increase
Heart rate change	decrease	decrease	no/slight
Stroke volume	increase	increase	increase
Cardiac output	no change	no change	increase
Active muscle blood flow	no change	increase	increase
Ventilation	no change	decrease	increase
VO2 difference	no change	slight increase	increase
Lactic acid levels	no change	decrease	increase

strength as you begin a workout regimen that involves resistance training (i.e., weight lifting). Early adaptations are almost entirely due to your neural pathways becoming familiar with the movements; they have little to do with gains in muscle. Weight training programs lasting 7 to 24 weeks generally increase the lean body mass by between .5 and 3%. For a 170-pound person, that means a gain of between .85 and 5.1 pounds.

In order for muscles to become stronger, they must break down. This is what causes soreness after working out. After lifting, your muscles will have micro-tears. It is during the recovery or resting that follows a workout that your body actually becomes stronger. The reason? Your muscle cells will try to adapt in order to handle the added stress you have placed on them, so those tears will be rebuilt bigger and stronger. This is why you should rest a day between intense workouts of body parts. For instance, if you do the bench press on Monday, you really shouldn't work your chest out again until at least Wednesday, so your muscles have time to heal and rebuild.

Bear in mind that, to maintain strength, you should perform strength-developing activities at least twice a week. You should perform at least 8 to 10 exercises that use the major muscle groups of legs, trunk, arms, and shoulders at each session, with 1 to 2 sets of 8 to12 reps of each exercise.

Health and Fitness Benefits of Aerobic Compared to Strength Training

Variable	Aerobic Exercise	Resistance Exercise
Resting blood pressure	↓↓	←→↓
Serum HDL cholesterol	↑↑	←→↑
Insulin sensitivity	↑↑	↑
Percent body fat	↓↓	↓
Bone mineral density	↑	↑↑↑
Strength	←→↑	↑↑↑
Physical function in old age	↑↑	↑↑↑
VO2max	↑↑↑	←→↑

Number of arrows refers to strength of scientific evidence, with three arrows indicating conclusive evidence. ↑ increase, ↓ decrease, ←→ no change

Free Weights vs. Machines

Once you do begin to lift, you will undoubtedly be confronted with the question of whether to use free weights (such as dumbbells) or machines. Here is a quick overview of the advantages and disadvantages of each:

Advantages of free weights:

- They use your body's own lever system, which requires the use of several muscles at once and allows you to work out in all three planes (frontal, sagittal, and horizontal).
- You will have a better transfer of training effect. For example, if you train on free weights and then test on a machine, you will perform better than those who train on machines then test on free weights.
- You can easily accomplish more large muscle group movements with free weights than machines, as there is more freedom of movement.
- Free weights allow a better standard of comparison, as a weight plate in one gym will weigh the same as a weight plate in another gym; whereas with machines too much relies on the calibration of the machine, and therefore the actual weight you are lifting can vary widely.

Advantages of machines:

- No skill is required to learn how to lift properly, because you are limited in movement; this is good for beginners.
- You can more easily isolate muscle groups, which can be helpful for injury prevention in and rehabilitation of specific areas.

Disadvantages of free weights:

- There is no dominant disadvantage, as long as you use common sense and take precautions, such as having a spotter.

Disadvantages of machines:

- They allow movement in only a single plane at a time, which does not relate to how movements are performed in real life: most movements you conduct on a daily basis require the ability to move through multiple planes at a time, and they require balance—neither of which happens with machines.
- There is little allowance for variations in how an exercise is conducted.
- Most machines are limited to performing only 1 to 2 different types of exercises.
- There is a limited range of weight increases. For example, lifting at 150 lbs may be too easy, whereas lifting at 162.5 lbs may be too hard, and there is no intermediate weight.

Exercises at High Intensity to Lose Weight/Burn Fat versus Low Intensity

You may have heard of the "sweet spot" in training at which the body burns more calories from fat than carbohydrates. In fact, many cardio machines have a setting for this intensity level, which you can select when exercising. This "sweet spot" does exist, and you can train at a level that will burn most calories from fat; however, to do so as a substitute for all other training is foolish.

As you read this, you are getting most of your energy by burning fat. At low intensities of exertion, your body prefers this fuel because it contains so much energy. Magazines sometimes mention that if you want to burn fat, you should train at low intensities. However, what you should be much more concerned about is the total calories you burn in an exercise session, not where those calories come from. Higher intensity training will burn more total calories, including some from fat, than a low-intensity workout. Check out these numbers:

Consider the following:

> When resting you burn around a calorie per minute, as opposed to 5 cal per minute walking. During that minute of rest you will burn 70% of that calorie from fat, or .7 calories, as opposed to 50% of the 5 cal from walking, or 2.5 calories of fat. So, although it is a lower percentage, the

> total fat burned in a minute is actually greater with the higher intensity exercise, and you will burn more total calories.

Think of it this way: would you rather have 10% of $1000, or 100% of $10? Furthermore, running two miles is as effective at burning calories as walking four miles at a moderate pace, and it takes about one quarter the time to accomplish.

Stretching and Warming Up

Here is an article on stretching that I wrote for my school's newsletter:

Calories burned during exercise: percentage of energy derived from fat:

Rest: 70%
Brisk walking: 50%
Jogging: 30%
All-out running: 0%

> From the time we first began little league sports, our coaches and parents told us that we would be wise to stretch before working out. Why? "Because it will help you limber up and prevent injuries," they said. However, research conducted over the past decade suggests otherwise. One prominent medical doctor who works for the Centers for Disease Control, Dr. Thacker, conducted a study that analyzed nearly 100 research articles on stretching and its relationship to injury prevention. His team concluded that stretching does increase flexibility, which is one of the five components of fitness, but the highest quality studies indicate that higher flexibility does not equate to fewer injuries. The fact is that few activities require extreme flexibility (think ballet or gymnastics). In the end he suggests that injuries could be more effectively prevented by more thorough warm-ups, strength training, and balancing drills than by stretching.
>
> Another well-known doctor, Ian Shrier, gives a few reasons why stretching shouldn't be expected to prevent injuries: 1) It doesn't change eccentric muscle activity (the kind that leads to soreness after a workout), 2) Improper stretching can actually cause much more harm than good, and 3) The stretching may mask pain, which can keep the exerciser from ignoring a pre-injury signal. He concludes that "The

basic science and clinical evidence today suggests that stretching before exercise is more likely to cause injury than prevent it."

Dr. Thacker states that "If the time you spend stretching causes you to lose time from something else—more running, strength training, or stability exercises—then you might be better off spending the time on that something else."

Furthermore, Robert Herbert Ph.D. and Marcos de Noronha Ph.D. concluded after analyzing 10 studies that stretching does not prevent soreness after exercise, either.

So what does this mean? Most exercisers would be wise to skip the stretching before exercise in favor of a better warm-up that is specific for the workout to follow. However, static stretching after exercise can increase flexibility, and therefore is encouraged.

The fact is, while flexibility remains a good thing, the effect of flexibility on exercise is still inconclusive. What is known is that you should not undertake flexibility exercises until the body is warm. Muscle, tendon, and ligament elasticity depends on blood saturation.

Benefits and Effects of Warm-up Before Strenuous Exercise

1. Increases breakdown of oxyhemoglobin, allowing greater delivery of oxygen to the working muscle.
2. Increases the release of oxygen from myoglobin.
3. Decreases the activation energy for vital cellular metabolic chemical reactions.
4. Decreases muscle viscosity, improving mechanical efficiency and power.
5. Improves speed of nervous impulses and augments sensitivity of nerve receptors.
6. Increases blood flow to muscles.
7. Decreases number of injuries to muscles, tendons, ligaments, and other connective tissues.
8. Improves the cardiovascular response to sudden, strenuous exercise (especially heart muscle blood flow).

9. Leads to earlier sweating, which reduces the risk of high body temperature during exercise.

So, what would be a good warm-up? Well, for starters, know that the time between warming up and actually performing should be minimal (less than a minute). An article from *Runner's World* that gives an idea of how to prepare for a race (such as the 2-miler you will do for the APFT), and which strongly relates to the endurance-based exercises the Army performs and can be adapted by making a few changes, offers this advice:

> 1. *To enhance performance*, your warm-up should involve at least 10 minutes of continuous activity—long enough for the muscles to reach their optimum temperature.
> 2. *The warm-up should elevate your heart rate* to about 70 to 80 percent of maximum. Less vigorous exercise doesn't seem to activate your cardiovascular system adequately, while more intense efforts can increase fatigue during the race.
> 3. *For competition lasting more than 60 minutes,* it's a good idea to interrupt your warm-up briefly, 10 to 15 minutes before the start, to take in about 10 ounces of sports drink. The carbohydrate in the drink will help you sustain your pace as your muscle glycogen begins to run low. (Also sip at least 5 ounces of sports drink every 15 minutes during the race—but make sure to practice all of this in training.)
> 4. *If you feel any muscle tightness* while you're warming up, stop jogging for a moment and stretch out the tight area (but don't count this stretching time as part of your 10-minute minimum). Studies confirm that this jog-stretch-jog combination can significantly improve the flexibility of muscles and connective tissues.
> 5. *As you begin to feel loose* and ready to race, visualize yourself running fast, particularly over the toughest portions of the course.
> 6. *Toward the end of the warm-up*, it's important to do a few 50- to 100-meter surges at approximately race pace. These surges "wake up" your nervous system and boost your coordination and efficiency.
> 7. *If your race takes place on a hot, humid day*, limit your warm-up to 10 minutes and try to do it in a shady area to decrease the risk of overheating.
> 8. *Even if it isn't hot out*, warm up for no more than 15 to 20 minutes.
> Follow the above guidelines before fast-paced workouts as well as races. Prior to less intense training sessions, you may not need to warm up, as you can gradually increase your pace during the workout. In effect, the first two miles of a moderately paced training run will act as the warm-up.

The above rules apply to all race distances of one mile or greater.

How can you adapt this to suit your workout? Simply make it more specific for the exercise you plan on performing. For example, the article suggests sprints before a race; so before a full workout or the APFT, you may be better off doing very brief bouts of push-ups or sit-ups. A good warm-up should be intense enough to increase the body's core temperature and cause some sweating.

What constitutes a good after-workout stretch? The American College of Sports Medicine suggests 2 to 4 repetitions of 15 to 30 seconds duration per stretch, 2 to 3 days a week. Your muscles should feel tight, but not painful. Be sure to research the stretches ahead of time to avoid potentially injury-inducing ones, such as rolling your neck.

The Importance of Movement

One of the most significant forces that drives blood throughout your body and back to the heart is the pumping effect of your muscles. During movement your muscles contract, squeezing together against your veins, pumping the blood to your heart with every step. This is why you should not suddenly stop exercising. For example, Howley and Franks state that "The recovery period between running intervals should include some work at a lower intensity (half your max) to help metabolize the lactate produced during the interval and to reduce the chance of cardiovascular complications that can occur when a person comes to a complete rest at the end of a strenuous exercise bout."

The cool-down after exercise should last between 5 and10 minutes. Doing this promotes faster recovery from fatigue and lets the leg muscle pump the blood back to the heart so it will not pool in the legs, which could cause delayed muscle stiffness and fainting and dizziness.

Back Pain

About 20% of medical discharges from the Army are due to lower back pain. At least 1/3 of sufferers have recurrent pain. The most prominent causes include:

- Poor posture
- Obesity
- Poor physical condition (muscular strength and flexibility)
- Smoking
- Psychological stress

Recommendations for prevention include:

- Exercise regularly the lower back and abs. Do not hyper-extend your back; this does not give it an extra workout, it just adds more stress on the spine.
- Lose weight, if applicable.
- Avoid smoking; it causes degenerative changes in the spine (nicotine degrades intervertebral disks).
- Avoid sitting/standing in one place too long.
- Practice good posture.
- Use a firm mattress. Lie on your back with a pillow under your knees, sleep on your side with legs bent and a pillow between your knees.
- Warm up thoroughly before exercise.
- Lift with your legs, not your back.

Theories on the cause of lower back pain center on the relationship between abdominal muscles and back muscles, and poor flexibility of the hamstring muscles and lower back. Weak muscles are easily fatigued and cannot support proper spine alignment. When standing, weak abs and inflexible hamstrings allow the pelvis to tilt forward. More evidence supports that low levels of musculoskeletal fitness predict recurrent low back pain. So, if you don't exercise because your back hurts, you increase the likelihood of hurting it again in the future. The best measure to take is prevention—by working out.

Flutter Kicks and Leg Raises

Again, below is an article I wrote for my battalion newsletter:

> At the beginning of last semester I requested that flutter kicks and leg lifts, as well as any exercise that closely resembles them, no longer be utilized as part of our battalion workouts. According to Dr. Michael Bird (Ph.D. in Exercise Science, with a specialization in Biomechanics), "Double leg-lifts are not good for the back of anyone, especially those with weak abdominal muscles or poor core strength. Other exercises can serve the same purpose without the associated risks. Flutter kicks are probably less risky than leg lifts, but not by much. . . . I would recommend other exercises that do not cause pelvic tilt and exaggerated lordosis curvature of the spine."
>
> What he means is that these exercises are mostly done by your iliopsoas muscles, which attach your spine to the front side of your femur (thigh bone). Lifting your legs while lying on your back causes the iliopsoas to contract, which pulls your legs up by anchoring on your spine. This, in turn, pulls your vertebrae forward, causing a condition known as lordosis, which is an unnatural curve of the back.

As the article states, doing exercises that involve raising your legs off the ground while the rest of your body lies on the ground will cause more harm than good. As discussed in the segment on lower back pain, injury to that region of the body causes multiple medical problems. Therefore, it makes sense to avoid undue strain on your lower back, especially when the disadvantages of doing such exercises significantly outweigh the advantages. Sticking with crunches, for example, is an effective and much safer alternative.

Spot Reduction

There are many rumors out there about how to trim the fat from specific body parts. These are ineffective. You cannot remove fat from one certain area. For example: doing crunches will not just remove the fat around your abdominal area, regardless of what infomercials might say. While it *will* make those muscles stronger, losing fat is a total-body process.

Slow-Motion Workouts

This is a concept that should be thoroughly understood to avoid wasting time in your workouts. Specificity is very important in training for anything. Therefore, it is almost worthless to do slow repetitions in your workouts. Often cadets in charge will do slow-count push-ups or over-head arm claps. They associate pain with an effective workout, but that is not always valid. Just because something is more difficult does not mean it is more beneficial. Training your muscles to perform tasks that they will never realistically do is pointless. Almost never will you find yourself in a situation where you are better off curling up in super slow motion, for example, than popping up at a normal, fast rate. Going slowly certainly will not help you on the APFT, where you must perform as many repetitions as possible in the allotted time. All workouts should be done quickly, yet with good form. Think of what you are training for, and tailor your workouts to resemble those actions.

The APFT Testing Flaw

The APFT assesses how many correct push-ups you can do in two minutes, how many correct sit-ups you can do in two minutes, and how quickly you can run two miles. The upside to this test is that it requires minimal personnel to conduct the testing, and the requirements for equipment are also minimal. These are the main reasons the Army continues to use it. However, the downside is that it does a poor job of meeting the principle of specificity. After all, would you rather have a soldier who can do 71 push-ups in two minutes but can bench press only 75% of his/her body weight, or one who can bench press at least 100% of his/her body weight 10 times, but can do only 60 push-ups in two minutes? I'd choose the bencher. Why? Because rarely, if ever, will the usefulness of your fitness in a combat environment come down to your chest endurance. Yet there are likely to be circumstances in which you will need to lift a heavy weight, such as a body, ruck, rocks, or vehicle parts. Likewise, how often will you be running two miles at a time with minimal clothing on? A timed ruck run with a specific weight load, or an obstacle course that tests agility and the ability to move objects (such as a casualty) would be a more practical and appropriate measure of cardio fitness.

About 15% of your national Order of Merit List (OML) score will be based on your APFT performance, therefore making it very important to train specifically for it. Just realize that in your post-cadet life it would be wise to do exercises that place less emphasis on high repetitions with minimal weight. Having said that, the best way to perform well on the APFT is to train at high reps with minimal rest between sets of sit-ups and push-ups, and to run high-intensity, long intervals on a track in addition to regular 3- to 4-mile runs for the two-mile test. Just be sure to adhere to the principles of exercise when planning your workouts.

On the day of the test, avoid eating before the test. At rest, blood flow to skeletal muscles is only about 21% of your total blood volume; most of your blood is in your gastrointestinal tract—your digestive system. During exercise blood shifts locations, so that up to 88% can be found in your muscles. This is why it's important not to eat before races or physical activity: because your food will just settle in your stomach. And without blood flowing to your digestive system, food can not be broken down and used for energy quickly.

Push-up Tips: to Increase Your Max

- Aim to reach a goal number of push-ups before stopping (example: 35 push-ups before you take your first break). After this break, do as many push-ups as you can while keeping good form. Once you become too fatigued to continue doing consecutive push-ups, start doing small sets of 3 to 5 at a time between short breaks.
- Throughout the workout, when you become fatigued, change your hand positioning, so the stress is spread between different muscles.
- Do 20+ push-ups after every time you use the bathroom.
- Lift weights at a gym.

Sit-up Tips: to Increase Your Max

- Unlike push-ups, try to do sit-ups at a steady pace. This includes not only movement but breathing.
- Try throwing yourself backward after you curl up, then pop back up. It takes more energy to move slowly.
- Once you reach initial fatigue (about halfway through the APFT), take a short break to let your muscles flush out some acid before continuing on.
- You have to train by doing full sit-ups—NOT crunches. Unlike the push-ups, which have several varieties, the sit-up has none. You must do extra, regular, full sit-ups to improve.

Sleep

The benefits of sleep include the following:

- Sleep helps your body repair itself and grow. During deep sleep your body releases hormones that help your body recover, fight off antibodies, and develop.
- Sleep reduces stress on your body by giving it time to relax.
- After a good rest you are better able to focus and remember information.

If three or more of the following describes you, it's possible you need more sleep:

- I need an alarm clock in order to wake up at the appropriate time
- It's a struggle for me to get out of bed in the morning
- I feel tired, irritable, and stressed out during the week
- I have trouble concentrating
- I have trouble remembering
- I feel slow with critical thinking, problem solving, and being creative
- I often fall asleep watching television
- I find it hard to stay awake in boring meetings or lectures, or in warm rooms

- I often nod off after heavy meals or a low dose of alcohol
- I often feel drowsy while driving
- I often sleep extra hours on weekend mornings
- I often need a nap to get through the day
- I have dark circles under my eyes

Some guidelines for sleep (from the Better Sleep Council and National Sleep Foundation):

- Maintain a regular sleep schedule for going to bed and waking up, including on weekends.
- Establish a regular, relaxing bedtime routine, such as soaking in a hot tub, then reading a book or listening to soothing music.
- Create a sleep-conducive environment that is dark, quiet, comfortable, and cool.
- Sleep on a comfortable mattress and pillows.
- Use the bedroom only for sleep and sex. It is best to keep work material, computers, and TV out of the bedroom.
- Finish eating at least 2 to 3 hours before bedtime.
- Exercise regularly. Scientific evidence confirms that people who exercise regularly and intensely do indeed spend more time in slow-wave sleep—a measure of sleep quality—than the inactive. But it is best to complete your workout at least a few hours before your bedtime.

Psychological Effects

There is always a lot more you can learn about health, wellness, and exercise. Do not be afraid to delve deeper into the chapter, do your own research, or contact an expert. But even after a quick reading of this brief treatment, the physiological aspects of fitness should be less of a mystery to you. Now that you are aware of the multitude of benefits that flow from better fitness—ranging from a better APFT score to a happier outlook on life to actually living longer—you can make wiser decisions. Exercising, when done properly, can lead to a slew of positive outcomes. Always ensure that your fitness program meets the criteria presented above, and you will be headed toward peak fitness in no time.

Summary of Relationship between Physical Activity and Psychological Health	
Self-esteem	↑↑
General sense of well-being	↑↑
Mood, vigor	↑↑
Cognition	↑
Depression	↓↓
Anxiety	↓↓

This figure summarizes the relationship between physical activity and psychological well-being, using current evidence. The strength of the relationship is represented by the arrows, with two arrows representing strong evidence in support and one arrow representing preliminary supporting evidence, with more research needed to confirm the association.

Chapter 3

Nutrition

Nutrition is important, for many reasons. It can have a bigger impact on controlling body weight than genes and exercise combined, and it will determine how much energy you have available. Appropriate nutrition can also lead to quick recovery and muscle growth after strenuous exertion. The following general tips and guidelines on eating properly can help you maximize your gains. Much of this material is straightforward, so little explanation is needed. Simply follow these instructions and you will optimize your diet. Remember: even regular endurance exercise will not fully counteract bad nutritional habits.

[Note: to convert from lb to kg: 1 lb/2.2= kgs]

General Guidelines

- 1g fat = 9 calories
  1g alcohol = 7 calories
  1g protein = 4 calories
  1g carbohydrate = 4 calories

- Most people consume the same 10 to 15 types of food each week, but try to expand your menu. Aim to eat at least 35 different foods every week.
- Do not substitute artificial food for real food if you can help it. While artificial foods such as protein bars can be convenient on the go, they do not contain the healthy phytochemicals and other protective qualities that real food has.
- To ensure that you are consuming enough vegetables, eat a big bowl of salad before dinner every evening. This salad should contain a variety of vegetables topped with little or no dressing. When choosing a dressing, make sure it is low calorie and low fat. Also, you should choose dark green, leafy vegetables over iceberg lettuce, and include bright-colored vegetables such as carrots, tomatoes, and bell peppers.
- The American Heart Association recommends eating oily fish every week. The type of fish *does* matter, with the three best choices—those with the highest healthy omega-3 fatty acids (the "good" fats)—being farmed Atlantic salmon, sardines in sardine oil, and wild Atlantic salmon.
- Iron is important to transport oxygen throughout your body. To enhance iron absorption, consume vitamin C with it. Conversely, drinking tea or coffee with a meal may inhibit iron absorption. It is better to drink those fluids before the meal rather than afterwards.
- Cereal is a great, convenient food and often contains plenty of fiber, vitamins, and minerals. If you are a cereal lover, aim for the following:

  —No more than 3 grams of fat per serving
  —No more than 250mg of sodium per serving
  —At least 5 grams of fiber per serving
  —No more than 8 grams of sugar per serving
  —At least 25% daily allowance of iron per serving

- Exercise does not increase vitamin needs, and they are NOT used up during exercise the same way carbohydrates are. Companies add vitamins to items such as Jelly Belly energy beans and sports drinks, but there is no scientific evidence behind their claims of speeding recovery or providing energy, and they offer no competitive advantage. Do not be stampeded into purchasing expensive potions claiming the contrary.

Fiber

- Male adults should consume 38 grams of dietary fiber each day; female adults should consume 25 grams daily.

Cholesterol

- To reduce LDL-C cholesterol (low-density lipoprotein, aka bad cholesterol, which is an indicator of cardiovascular disease):

  —Reduce consumption of dietary saturated fats (especially meat and dairy fats) and trans fatty acids
  —Reduce body weight (or maintain normal body weight)
  —Reduce intake of dietary cholesterol (found in all animal products)
  —Increase intake of whole-grain carbohydrates and dietary water-soluble fibers (especially fruits, vegetables, beans, and oat products)

- To increase HDL-C (high-density lipoprotein, aka good cholesterol):

  —Perform aerobic exercise at least 90 minutes a week
  —Reduce weight, aiming for leanness
  —Do not smoke
  —If you consume alcohol, do so moderately

Multivitamins

Most food nowadays is fortified; think cereal, bread, and even the chocolate powder that makes chocolate milk. In these circumstances, as long as you follow an effective diet, vitamin pills—with the possible exception of vitamin D—are essentially a waste of money. Consuming extra vitamins (more than 100% of the recommended amount) will not help you recover more quickly, stay healthier, or give you energy. In addition, if you rely on the pills you miss out on other important chemicals that help the body that are found in actual foods such as fruit and vegetables. These include arytenoids, falconoids and isolators, and protease inhibitors. Having said that, you can safely take a multivitamin as an insurance policy or for peace of mind, so long as you do not over-consume the recommended amount of vitamins and minerals.

Recommended Dietary Carbohydrate (CHO) Intake

- First, to be clear: carbohydrates per se are NOT fattening. It is excessive calories in any form (fats, carbs, protein, alcohol) that are fattening. Your body needs carbohydrates to exercise because it is by far the preferred source of energy during activity. Do not cheat your body by consuming too few carbs and too much fat and protein.
- A CHO-rich diet (6 to 10g/kg/day) can help prevent glycogen depletion. For example: A 150-pound person would need to consume about 544g per day (150lb=68kg. 68kg x 8g= 544g of CHO)
- If an individual exercises intensely for less than one hour a day, 6 to 7 g/kg body weight/day may replenish glycogen stores.
- For the individual who exercises for several hours a day, 8 to 10 g/kg body weight/day is required.
- Active individuals should meet a minimum of 60% of their total daily caloric requirement with CHO.
- Trained individuals are able to store more CHO in their muscles (about 20 to 50% more) than untrained individuals, which means they can last longer when exercising. Consequently, carb loading before an event will be much more effective for that trained individual.

Muscle Glycogen per 100 Grams (3.5 oz) of Muscle	
Untrained muscle	13g
Trained muscle	32g
Carbohydrate-loaded muscle	35-40g

Classic Active Diet

- 55 to 65% CHO, 25 to 30% fats, 15 to 20% protein.
- Getting enough CHO can be difficult. Eating too much can cause gastrointestinal stress, and exercise can suppress appetite. Liquids can be an easy solution. A simple homemade shake can be constructed from skim milk, low-fat ice cream, and 2 packs of Carnation Instant Breakfast. Such a drink would measure about 24 oz and contain 520 Kcal, with 220g CHO, for about $1.35. In addition, it would have 18g of protein and only 7g of fat.

Carb Loading

- Prior to endurance events, most athletes saturate their muscles with carbohydrates in order to provide lasting energy during the upcoming physical exertion. You can apply this same principle very effectively to ruck marches, land navigation, and a number of other military training events. Note that you don't need to exercise to a complete depletion of stores of carbohydrates before beginning this process. In fact, over the two weeks before such an event, you should taper off from exercise in order to let your muscles rest and repair.
- One effective way to carb load:

—For three days, consume CHO for 50% of your total caloric intake.

—Follow that with three days of CHO intake at 70% of total calories.

- Water stores with glycogen, so you will feel "heavy" during loading. An easy way to tell if you have carbo loaded properly is to weigh yourself. If you have gained 2 to 4 pounds, then you are doing well. For every ounce of CHO stored, three ounces of water is stored along with it. This water becomes available during exercise and helps fight off dehydration and regulate your body temperature.
- To avoid intestinal problems, you may wish to make the lunch the day prior to your event your big meal, and consume a smaller dinner, which will allow plenty of time for the food to digest.
- Choose familiar foods. Do not eat only fruit because it will cause diarrhea. Likewise, too much white bread will cause constipation.

Fats

- It is easier for your body to convert fat into body fat than it is to convert carbs into body fat. While it takes 23% of ingested calories to convert excess carbs into body fat, it only costs the body 3% of ingested excess fat calories to convert them to body fat.
- Lipid intake should not exceed 30% of calories.
- Unsaturated fats should account for 70 to 80% of total fat intake (equally distributed between polyunsaturated and monounsaturated fats).
- Saturated fats should be less than 10% of total fat intake.
- The total daily cholesterol intake should be less than 300mg.

Protein

- Perhaps because of its nutritional importance, or perhaps because muscle tissue is composed of it, protein has taken on an almost mystical power in athletic circles, causing individuals who are very athletically active to over-consume it.
- There is no good evidence that very high protein intakes (>2g/kg body weight/day) are either necessary or beneficial.

- In the absence of heavy resistance training, excess protein does not build more muscle.
- Excessively high protein intake will result in the conversion of protein to CHO and/or fat, which will be stored when it exceeds the energy requirement; this causes weight gain.
- The removal of nitrogen from protein via the kidneys can cause dehydration; individuals consuming extra protein must maintain an above-average fluid intake.
- For physically active individuals, there is little need for a long-term increase in protein intake, although an intake of 1.3 to 1.6g/kg body weight/day (1g/.5lb body weight/day: 68g extra protein per day for a 150-lb person) is recommended—even when carbo loading.
- For individuals performing heavy resistance training, a slightly greater-than-normal protein intake (1.7-1.8 g/kg body weight/day) might promote muscle mass gains. The average American diet already contains that much.
- Endurance athletes need protein in their diet (1.3-1.6 g/kg body weight/day) as well. During endurance events about 5% of energy can come from protein sources.

Water

- *Takeaway: 1% dehydrated = 5% decrease in performance.* Your heart will have to beat 3 to 5 times more every minute to compensate for this dehydration. At 3% dehydration your aerobic ability will be significantly impaired.
- Athletes should prehydrate by consuming adequate fluids before an event. The total should be about 2-3 mL per pound (5-7 mL per kg). Prehydration should begin 24 hours ahead of time, but no less than four hours prior to the activity. About 2 hours before exercise drink three glasses (about 17 ounces) of fluid to ensure adequate hydration and allow time for excretion of excess ingested water. Drink another cup 5 to 10 minutes before the start of the event.
- While performing intense exercise, individuals may lose as much as 2 L/hr, a rate that cannot be matched by water intake.

Adverse Effects of Dehydration	
% Body Wt Loss	Symptoms
1.0	Thirst threshold
2.0	Stronger thirst, vague discomfort, loss of appetite
3.0	Increasing hemoconcentration, dry mouth, reduction in urine
4.0	Decrement of 20-30% in exercise capacity
5.0	Difficulty in concentrating, headache, impatience
6.0	Severe impairment of exercise temperature regulation, increased respiration, extremity numbness and tingling
7.0	Likely collapse, if combined with heat and exercise

- To minimize risk of thermal injury and impairment of performance during exercise, fluid replacement should equal fluid loss.
- Only about 1/3 to 2/3 of the fluid lost during exercise is replaced on a voluntary basis.
- Thirst typically lags behind the body's requirement for water. By the time you're thirsty, you've lost 2% of your body weight and are dehydrated.
- Alcohol and excessive caffeine drinks act as diuretics, which remove more water than they contribute. However, just a cup of coffee will not dehydrate your body.
- Caffeine has been shown to boost performance, though more may not be better. Aim for about 1.5 milligrams per pound (3 milligrams per kg) of body weight.
- In general, plain water is the best way to replenish fluids required by the body.
- For exercise lasting <1 hour, water is the best replacement fluid.
- For exercise >1 hour, CHO and electrolytes may be added to the solution (sports drinks).

- Sports drinks should have a relatively low sodium concentration (.5-.7g Na/L) and limited CHO levels (4%-8%). Because they are very dilute, they leave the stomach during activity quicker than calorie-dense drinks. However, they lack a sufficient amount of electrolytes and carbohydrates to be an effective after-workout recovery drink. After activity, try chocolate milk rather than Gatorade, for example.
- Colder air contains less moisture, so greater fluid volumes leave the respiratory tract (i.e., through breathing), as much as 1 L/day.
- Cold weather stimulates greater urine output by the kidneys, so fluid replacement is just as important in winter as in summer for active people.
- When properly hydrated, you should be urinating every 2 to 4 hours. The urine itself should be very pale in color.
- Can body temperature be controlled and dehydration prevented by wetting the head and skin during exercise? Although skin wetting may be psychologically pleasing, researchers have found that it does not reduce sweat volume or core body temperature. It is far better to drink the water.

Over-Training Syndrome

Sometimes soldiers, like athletes, over-train, which leaves them unable to recover quickly enough from their workouts. Such over-training will actually cause a reversal of the physical and mental strengths you have worked so hard to develop. It may lead to pain that doesn't go away, irritability, persistent fatigue, and other ailments. Here's how to combat it:

- 3 to 4 hours before exercise, consume an easily digestible, CHO-rich solid meal yielding 5g CHO/kg body weight.
- 1 to 1.5 hours before exercise, consume a CHO-rich drink (12 to 16 oz) yielding 1 g CHO/kg body weight.
- Following exercise (within 30 min), consume a CHO-rich drink or energy bar. (Note: bagels and fat-free Fig Newtons are as effective as expensive bars.)

- Later (1 to 4 hours after exercise), consume an easily digested, high-CHO meal supplemented with a CHO-rich drink or concentrated source (e.g., energy bar, Fig Newtons, bagels).

The Pre-Competition Meal

- As a general rule, you need 3 to 4 hours to digest a large meal, 2 to 3 for a smaller meal, 1 to 2 for a blended or liquid meal, and less than an hour for a small snack.
- An 8 to 12 hour period without eating may significantly deplete CHO reserves in a performer.
- Extra protein may speed dehydration.
- Liquid meals may be good, especially in day-long competitions, since they leave little residual bulk in the intestines.
- Around four hours before competition, you should consume 2 g CHO/lb body weight (4 g per kg) along with one to two glasses of water. The meal should consist of rapidly digestible, low-fiber starch (e.g., Cream of Wheat hot cereal, white bread, bagels, pasta, refined cereals). This way the stomach should be empty by the time of competition, so as to avoid uncomfortable feelings of fullness or cramping. You can consume .5 g of CHO/lb body weight (1 g per kg) an hour before exercise.

Food on the Go

- For dry items, try: Bagels, Fig Newtons, pop tarts, pretzels, crackers, dried fruit, fresh fruit, trail mix, individual cereal boxes, juice boxes or bottles, power bars.
- For cooler items: Yogurt, canned fruit, jelly, juices, skim milk (protein), rice pudding, sliced turkey (protein), low-fat cheese, cut-up vegetables.

Eating on Game Day

- Eat something the morning of the event. This will ensure that you have an adequate blood sugar level. Though your muscles store glycogen for energy, your brain does not. Without a food source near the time of the event, your brain will not have the fuel it needs to properly function and provide the mental drive required to be successful.

- All-day sports events: Proteins and fats move through the digestive system slowly and may impair performance.
- In order to properly refuel from one bout of intense activity to another, consume at least .5 grams of CHO per pound (1g per kg) body weight every two hours for four to six hours. Also consume some fat and protein to aid in recovery.
- <1 hour between events: Get CHOs in a liquid form (juices or sports drinks).
- If solids are required, eat fruit (oranges, peaches, bananas, or pears).
- Limit the quantity of food to avoid the "too full" feeling.
- 2 to 3 hours between events: Add some solid CHOs to the diet (bagel, English muffin, hot or cold cereal) along with some fruit.
- Drink fluids (water is best, but CHO drinks are good too).
- Eat early in the interval to allow digestion.
- Again, limit the quantity of food.
- 4 to 6 hours between events: The athlete may eat a small meal composed mostly of CHOs.
- A small sandwich, some spaghetti (light on sauce), some bread (no butter), and a sports drink (or water) will not sit in the stomach like a rock.
- Don't eat at the concession stand; it's mostly protein and fat.
- 10 to 12 hours between events: Avoid the high-fat, high-protein "reward" meal for doing well on the competition's first day.
- Select high-CHO meals that will be easily digestible overnight or throughout the day.
- Select fruit as dessert rather than high-fat stuff.
- Rehydrate!
- Remember: The meal after a major competition is as important as the pre-game meal; it should be high in CHOs to reload glycogen stores.
- A snack during long exercise workouts (60-90 min) may help performance.

To Gain Weight

- Heavy resistance training supported by adequate energy replacement (700 to 1000 extra Kcal/day) and protein intake (1.5 g/kg body weight) coupled with sufficient recovery will increase muscle mass.
- Aim to consume protein and carbohydrates every 3 to 4 hours. A sufficient calorie supply may ensure that protein is used for muscle growth and not metabolized for energy. When amino acid levels are high, they are more readily consumed by the muscle, causing muscle growth, and the carbs give the muscle energy so it won't have to break down the protein for fuel.
- Approximately 3,500 Kcal from a well-balanced diet are required to gain one pound of muscle.
- Eat calorie-dense foods.
- Eat rapidly to get ahead of the satiety signal.
- Eat regularly (don't skip meals).
- Eat snacks between meals.
- Use fruit juices to enhance caloric intake rather than drinking, say, water.
- The protein and amino acids in ordinary foods are just as, if not more, effective than those found in supplements. On a per gram basis, supplements often cost 2 to 4 times as much as ordinary food, plus they may lack vitamins, minerals, and yet-to-be-discovered bioactive nutrients found in food. Rather than eating a protein bar, try nuts, fish, or dairy products.

The Protein-Carb Combo

- The "window" for most effective response of trained muscle is in the first 15 to 60 minutes after the exercise session.
- Protein causes additional increase in circulating insulin and growth hormones.
- Carbohydrate-rich foods and fluids should be ingested soon after long-term exercise, until at least 8 to 10 grams CHO/kg body weight are consumed. Aim for 1 g per kg body weight every hour, taken at thirty minute intervals for 4 to 5 hours.

- Post-exercise meals should consist of high Glycemic Index (GI) carbohydrates to enhance glycogen resynthesis. High-GI foods break down more quickly, and the energy is more readily made available to the body.
- The addition of protein to a carbohydrate supplement immediately after working out may create a hormonal environment more conducive to muscle gain.
- With the protein-carb combo, the process of replenishing glycogen to depleted muscles may accelerate, speeding recovery.

Glycemic Index of Some Common Foods

High (GI > 100)	GI	Moderate (GI = 60-100)	GI	Low (GI < 60)	GI
Instant Rice	128	Muffin	88	Spaghetti	59
Rice Chex®	127	Oatmeal	87	Apple juice	58
Crispix® cereal	124	Ice Cream	87	Tomato soup	54
Baked Potatoes	121	Rice	80	Apple	52
Cornflakes	119	Oatmeal Cookies	79	Yogurt, low fat	47
Corn Chex®	118	Corn	78	Dried apricots	44
Sucrose	117	Banana	76	Kidney beans	42
Waffles	109	Orange Juice	74	Peach, fresh	40
Doughnuts	108	Chocolate	70	Whole milk	39
Honey	104	Lactose	65	Red lentils	36
Bagels	103	Orange	62	Fructose	32
Carrots	101	Grapes	62	Soy beans	25

NOTE: The glycemic index fluctuates from person to person and meal to meal, and depends on the combination of foods. Adhering to a diet that is based on the index is not recommended, as simply eating healthy foods will produce the same result.

- To emphasize the importance of carbohydrates, consider this: if, after exercising, you consume a CHO-only diet, you will recover in about 45 minutes. If, on the other hand, you consume a protein-and-fat-only diet, it will take you days to recover.
- Recipe for a homemade smoothie: one pack of Carnation Instant Breakfast, 8 oz skim milk, 1 banana, 1 tbs of peanut butter. = 414 Kcal, 70g CHO, 10 g fat, 17g protein.
- Recipe for a homemade shake: two packs of Carnation Instant Breakfast, 8 oz skim milk, 8 oz light ice cream. = 699 Kcal, 102g CHO, 18g fat, 40g protein.

Weight Loss

Diet has a stronger impact on weight loss than any other factor. The key to losing weight is to simply consume fewer calories than you burn; if you do so, you will lose weight (provided that you do not have a metabolic problem). Be wary of consuming rewarding foods after a hard workout. Consider this: it takes running about two miles to burn 200 calories. Depending on how fit you are, this can take between 12 and 20 minutes. But it only takes a couple of minutes to consume the 270 calories in a Snickers Bar.

Choosing a Safe and Successful Weight-Loss Program

Many overweight people lose weight on their own without entering a weight-loss program. Others need the social and professional support that commercial weight-loss programs provide. Almost any of the commercial weight-loss programs can work in the short term, but they may not promote safe and healthy habits that can be followed over the long term.

What elements of a weight-loss program should one look for in judging its potential for safe and successful weight loss? Look for these features:

- *Provides or encourages food intake that exceeds 1,200 calories per day for a woman and 1,600 calories per day for a man.* Diets recommending less than these amounts, even for most overweight and obese individuals, are not recommended because they are typically low in essential vitamins and minerals and can lead to excess muscle loss and lower metabolism.

- *Provides safe nutrition.* It should include all the vitamins and minerals at recommended intake levels. Although low in calories, it should be based on the food guide pyramid, providing servings from all the recommended food groups. High-protein diets are not recommended. Weight-loss diets should promote health, not harm.
- *Promotes a safe and realistic weight loss of 1 to 2 pounds per week.* Good weight-management programs don't promise or imply dramatic, rapid weight loss. Don't seek a "quick fix," because the quicker the weight comes off, the quicker it goes back on. Although not as appealing, slow and gradual weight loss is more effective.
- *Does not attempt to make one dependent on special products that are sold for a profit.* The best programs emphasize wise choices from the traditional food supply and feature supermarket and restaurant tours and cooking schools to teach you how to improve your food selection and meal preparation. Learn how to improve eating habits within the context of your own social, cultural, and income background.
- *Does not promote or sell products that are unproven or spurious.* Companies sell a wide array of weight-loss products that have little if any value, including starch blockers, grapefruit pills, sauna belts, body wraps, ear staples, and hormone releasers.
- *Is led by a qualified instructor.* Health-promotion professionals, registered dieticians, and physicians specializing in weight control are qualified to direct weight-control programs. Check out the experience and credentials of the weight-control program leaders before signing up.
- *Includes a maintenance phase.* It is difficult to change behaviors that have formed over many years. Relapse often occurs during stressful life events. Weight-control programs

should provide support on a regular basis for at least one year after one has lost weight.
- *Emphasizes a lifestyle approach.* Good programs include guidance on exercise, diet, and behavior change that are continued for a lifetime, not just the duration of the program.

Smoking

At rest, and to a degree during exercise, nicotine from smoking cigarettes increases the heart rate and blood pressure, decreases the heart's output, and increases the oxygen demands of the heart muscle. Smoking increases the resistance of airflow in the lung passageways, making it harder to deliver oxygen to the lungs during subsequent exercise. Nicotine also increases lactate levels in the blood during exercise, which, when it rises high enough, can make people feel fatigued or feel like quitting exercise.

When smokers abstain from smoking for as little as one week, exercise performance improves.

Chapter 4

Garrison

At field training exercises (FTXs), joint field training exercises (JFTXs), and Leadership Development and Assessment Course (LDAC), you will be evaluated on your leadership while on a base or indoors; that environment is called garrison. Leadership there is different than leadership out in the field, in that you will focus more on time limits and punctuality ("hacks") and proper uniform and less on correct tactics.

The following items constitute some "quick-hit" advice for making sure that you perform at a high level in garrison—and get credit for it.

Disseminate Information Quickly

While in garrison you will usually have little time to complete tasks. Therefore it is vital to quickly break down the operations order (OPORD) given to you by Higher (i.e., higher authority) and disseminate that information to your squad/platoon. You will be taught about the 1/3-2/3 rule for time management, but realistically you should be striving to get any information out to your subordinates as soon as possible. You can always fill in the changes and specifications later. In the real Army there will be plenty of time to plan actions, but as a cadet you need to focus on letting everyone know, as quickly as you can, what is required and when.

Keep Accountability

If there is one thing that makes you look really bad in front of cadre (the military officers, noncommissioned officers (NCOs), and contractors who teach and guide you), it's not maintaining accountability of your squad or platoon. Accountability simply means knowing how many cadets you have present, who is missing, where they are, and why.

But that can easily be fixed. Any time you are stopped or you are in formation, do a quick check to ensure that all of your cadets are accounted for. Using your subordinate leaders, such as your team leaders when you are the squad leader, to help you out is the most effective way to keep tabs on your unit. You should delegate to your subordinates as often as possible—but you remain responsible.

After Action Review (AAR)

AARs will be conducted after each significant training event, either at the platoon or squad level. You will discuss what was supposed to happen, what did happen, sustains, and improves. (Sustains are what went well and should be continued in the future, and improves are what went wrong and should be adjusted.) Often in garrison you will not be asked to conduct a squad-level AAR, but go ahead and do one on your own anyway. This allows the squad to improve itself, and it shows the cadre that you are taking the initiative to improve yourself.

Schedules

If you will be in a garrison environment for an extended period (most likely just at LDAC), make task schedules for the platoon. Write out a rotation that dictates which squads will be doing which tasks during barracks cleaning, the order of who gets to eat first for each meal, who gets to do laundry, and who will be pulling fire guard duty (security) in the middle of the night. This will maintain order and prevent favoritism.

Hip-Pocket Training

This is the training that you do on the fly when you find you have a half hour to kill and there are no planned activities. Focus this training on either that day's or the following day's activities. These are areas of knowledge that you should know, and that you should be able to teach on any given day. Some ideas: first aid; searching an enemy prisoner of war (EPW); conducting a Field Leadership Reaction Course (FLRC) scenario; and calling in a medical evacuation. Never get caught with your squad lying around doing nothing.

Take Initiative

This applies to any type of training, in any environment. Be proactive: always seek to take action, rather than waiting for things to come to you. If the squad mentions some kind of problem, no matter how small, go ahead and actively seek a solution. The less you have to be told by Higher to do something that you know you'll have to do eventually, the better.

Yellow Cards

At the end of every day you are in garrison, you will have to write out a yellow card. It records everything you accomplished that day. During the day write down notes of everything you do; you may think you'll be able to remember it all, but you won't. Do not lie on your card about anything.

It is especially important to write a strong card because the cadre evaluating you will not be able to watch you all day, so they will review your yellow card. Don't hesitate to use the yellow card to let the cadre know exactly what you did.

Receiving counseling after completing a mission

When you're in charge, try to incorporate activities that encompass each leadership dimension. Then, while writing the card, write in detail about specific instances when you displayed each of those dimensions. This makes your yellow card strong. Writing a good yellow card could easily mean the difference between being rated "excellent" and "satisfactory."

Use Visual Aids

When briefing your OPORDs in garrison, always try to incorporate visual aids. This can be as simple as using an alcohol pen to write out the timeline on a locker or drawing a picture on a large piece of paper so cadets can visualize where the training and movement will take place.

Don't be afraid to go all out. One cadet demonstrated what the next day's uniform would be by dressing up in it, including the face paint.

Being First Sergeant (1SG) at Camp

Here are some helpful tips.

- Know how many cadets should be in each platoon.
- Have Platoon Sergeants (PSGs) get weapons/squad accountability and put their platoons at parade rest before you call "Fall in" and/or call the company to attention.
- Only order "Fall in" for the first formation of the day.
- BE LOUD!
- Meet with the PSGs throughout the day to keep them informed on everything.
- Check sensitive items (key equipment, such as weapons) before any movement to ensure that nothing has been lost or stolen.
- Meet with PSGs after the Commanding Officer (CO) briefs the OPORD to assign specific tasks and set the tone for your expectations.
- Your goal should be for all PSGs to get Es (excellent evaluations).
- Make a list of all the detail duties for each platoon and keep track of which ones you give to each platoon. That way you can make sure you are fair, and can prove to the PSGs that they are not being given unfair loads.

While garrison duty may not be as exciting as field exercises, you will spend a lot of time in garrison, and it provides excellent opportunities to practice leadership and attention to detail. By practicing these tips you will be well prepared for any leadership position.

Chapter 5

Land Navigation

Doing land navigation can be very stressful for cadets. A large chunk of the cadet's grade usually depends on how well he or she performs, and it's one of the few activities in which the cadet is on his/her own.

Land nav (as it is often called) consists of being given a map, pencil, compass, protractor, and eight-digit coordinates, then using those tools to reach points the cadre have set up in the surrounding terrain that correspond to the coordinates on the map. Typically you will have five hours to find up to eight particular points assigned to you during the day and three hours to find up to five points at night. Other cadets will be assigned the same number of points to find, but theirs will be in different locations, so not every cadet will be walking the same path to the same point at the same time.

Your cadre will go over how to conduct land navigation in detail, but the following are a few helpful pointers.

Conducting land navigation to find distance and direction to objective

Don't Panic

Much too often a cadet who is having trouble finding a point will begin to panic. This comes from the stress of needing to perform well, coupled with frustration and the possibility of being lost. The first step is to simply pause and take a moment to settle down.

The second step to realize is that it's not uncommon to get off your azimuth (the direction you were headed), which can lead you off your desired course. But your situation is recoverable.

So begin looking around you for some noticeable feature. This could be a trail, a hill, or a pond, for instance. Find that new terrain feature on the map. Then shoot a new azimuth from there to where your point should be.

Land Navigation is Not a Race

Many cadets get too caught up in thinking that they need to rush, both when plotting their points and hurrying to those points. While there does need to be a sense of urgency, it's unwise to go too fast. When plotting points it is better to measure twice and plot once than to hurriedly plot a point and go into the woods and get lost, only to realize that you didn't plot the point correctly. This eats up much more time than simply taking a few minutes to recheck plotting, distance, and direction. Also, rushing is likely to throw off your pace count (how many steps it takes you to walk 100 meters), which is the only means you have available to keep track of distance.

Rather, focus on doing everything correctly the first time, then move with a sense of urgency. If you're not the first back, it's not a big deal. As long as you're back in time, finding all the points is finding all the points, whether it takes you three hours or four and a half hours.

Try to Find All of the Points

As previously noted, you typically will be tasked to find 13 points total (eight for the day, five for the night). But keep searching for points until time is out or you've found all of them. Always try to find *every* point because:

- the more points you find, the better your grade (and your national OML ranking) will be.
- often cadets find a point in the woods that they *think* is the one they're looking for, but really it's not. A cadet may go out at night, find three points, and decide to head back to camp. Upon return, he (or she) may be told that one of the points found was not assigned to him, so he really found only two. Since passing land nav requires finding at least the minimum number of day and night points, he will have failed. Don't let that happen to you!

Chapter 6

Field Leadership Reaction Course (FLRC)

During the FLRC you will be presented with a number of items, consisting of various materials and obstacles, that constitute both tools and challenges. For example, you may be given a couple of boards, a rope, and a barrel, and be directed to get the barrel to the other side of a creek that the boards are too short to reach across. The course tests how quickly you can plan for and adapt to unexpected circumstances.

However, you are likely to receive training on and get an opportunity to practice many of these challenges before you go to the Leadership Development and Assessment Course (LDAC). Therefore only a few tips appear below.

3D Terrain Models

Whenever possible (which is almost always), make a three-dimensional (3D) terrain model of the obstacle your squad is about to navigate, to use when briefing your operations order (OPORD). This is valuable because it's hard to explain concepts of

Planning how to traverse an FLRC obstacle

traversing some obstacles using only a 2D diagram. And 3D modeling is much more practical on the FLRC course than, say, on a Situational Training Exercise (STX) lane (see next chapter), because the FLRC covers just one area.

So make sure you have with you a few nails, yarn, and whatever other props you feel may come in handy; but don't be afraid to use items from your surroundings, including rocks and sticks.

Don't Tell the Squad Leader What to Do

The key to FLRC is teamwork. The focus of the exercise is on the squad leader (SL), so if you are acting as a member of the squad, you are not being evaluated. You can suggest to the SL—quite openly, as long as you're tactful—what he or she should do. But if he doesn't like your recommendation and decides to follow a different course of action, let it go—and don't make a big deal out of it. (Because during FLRC everyone is in a confined area, everyone is likely to hear whatever you decide to say.) It's the SL's lane, and he should run it as he sees fit. One way to look bad to both fellow cadets and cadre, during *any* activity, is to step on their toes and *tell* them what they should do.

Treat it Like a Real Mission

Too often cadets let their discipline slide while doing FLRC lanes; don't be one of them. Always actively listen during the briefing of the OPORD, give five-paragraph OPORDs yourself (see Appendix B), and remain "tactical" (i.e., in an operational mindset).

Crossing the FLRC obstacle

Chapter 7

Situational Training Exercises (STX)

Situational training exercises (STX, pronounced "sticks") are a key training element, a cornerstone of cadet life in the field. At camp you will experience four straight 12-hour days of STX lanes.

What is a STX lane? Basically, it's a mini-mission designed to test your ability to plan thoroughly, exercise your judgment, and lead others. You will be called aside by your tactics officer (TAC), along with your recorder (a fellow cadet you designate to help you take notes). Your TAC will read to you the platoon operations order (OPORD), and you will jot down as much of the relevant information as you can in the limited time available. Next you will break it down to the squad level: you will make a plan for how to execute the mission, and brief that plan to your squad. Then you will execute it.

Don't worry too much: your school will help prepare you for STX by educating you on what is contained in an OPORD, how to make terrain model kits (TMKs), and how to conduct missions in general. What follows are guidelines on how to do well at STX lanes once you are in charge (likely sometime during your junior year) and at

Receiving the mission (above) and conducting recon (below)

Leadership Development and Assessment Course (LDAC). Much of what is mentioned here also applies to patrolling lanes (discussed in the next chapter), so don't be afraid to use these guidelines during those missions as well.

Don't Stress Out Over SOPs

Standard operating procedures (also called standing operating procedures, or SOPs) are important to how a squad functions. An SOP lays out how the squad should proceed under various circumstances. For example, you may have a squad SOP for how to cross a linear danger area (LDA), such as a road.

However, don't get too caught up in creating and hashing out SOPs. You really only need to establish SOPs for actions that are both common and complex, such as crossing an LDA and using hand signals. For everything else, just let the person in charge (the squad leader) designate what he or she wants during a particular OPORD. He'll be more comfortable doing things the way he wants to, he'll be able to explain things well, and he'll come across as knowledgeable in front of the cadre. It also saves the squad time otherwise spent arguing about whose way of doing something is best.

Have a Timeline

This is not the same as the timeline that you may issue with your OPORD; rather, this covers your planning phase. It dictates how long you should spend on each segment of preparation: receiving the mission, making a plan, issuing the plan, rehearsing, and conducting pre-combat inspections (PCIs). By knowing where you should be at any given time, you will know when to move to the next stage and when to slow down or speed up. It will ensure that you have enough time to get each of those important steps completed. A recommended timeline is as follows:

Pulling security as a buddy team

- 0-5 min—*Receive the OPORD*
- 5-20 min—*Issue the warning order* (WARNO; a preliminary OPORD) and plan the OPORD (This is when the special teams should rehearse)
- 20-30 min—*Issue the OPORD*
- 30-40 min—*Conduct rehearsals* (Include actions on the objective (see Glossary), crossing an LDA, etc.)
- 40-45 min—*Conduct PCIs* (Make sure everyone has full canteens, there are no dangling straps on rucks, everyone has proper camouflage, etc. A good test is to have everyone jump up and down with their rucks three times to see if anything makes any undue noise.)

Remain Tactical

During the mission always remain tactical—even if the rest of your squad doesn't. Not only is it good training, but it sets you apart and your TACs and peers will notice. This includes taking a knee or going prone whenever you're stopped (depending on how long you stop for and your unit SOP), maintaining appropriate spacing while moving, and observing noise discipline. (See the Glossary for more discussion of this concept.)

In addition, know when to utilize various tactics. For instance, when crossing open terrain you should not just run across. Rather, bound (i.e., leap-frog), so that half your unit can perform overwatch security while the other half moves to a covered/concealed position. In addition, make sure there is always rear security. This means looking around and behind you during movement, watching your back during the leader's recon, and keeping eyes on what is going on away from the objective while the special teams perform their tasks.

Make Sure Special Teams are Prepared

You will be able to save a significant amount of time on the objective simply by having the special teams prepare ahead of time. This includes having them write out as much of a medical evacuation 9-line message as possible while still in the assembly area (AA). (For a sample 9-line MEDEVAC message, see Appendix H.)

Pulling security

Know How to Write an OPORD

The trick to being able to write a good OPORD quickly is to have a skeleton already jotted out in your notebook, with plenty of space to

Pulling security

Support by fire element in position to attack

take notes. This will save you from having to rewrite anything and will ensure that you copy all necessary information.

Once you have the times, go ahead and convert your H-hours to date-time groups. For example, if H-hour (the time your mission begins) is 1530 and you must be on the objective by H + 80, and it's February 3rd, 2010, you'd say something like this: "4th squad will seize the objective no later than (NLT) 031650FEB10."

For a sample patrolling OPORD, see Appendix B.

Map Recon

As you prepare your OPORD, take time to look at the map and get an idea of the terrain you will be facing. Include this information in your briefing. Not only will this let your squad know whether to expect LDAs or dense brush, it will also show your evaluator that you are prepared.

Terrain Model Kit (TMK)

There are a few tricks you can use to make exceptional terrain models for your squad leader when you're the recorder. Doing so

Pulling security while leaders issue a WARNO

better clarifies what exactly is supposed to happen, and it's a way to show that you are a competent cadet.

- Clear the area for the TMK. This means removing all sticks, grass, leaves, and rocks. You want the area as plain and flat as possible to start with. Frame the area with sticks.
- Dump out all contents of your TMK, and use every piece you possibly can. This is much more time-efficient than digging through your bag for each piece; and the more pieces you use, the more specific and clear the terrain model will be.
- Mark off one corner of the cleared area to do a blown-up model of the objective. This allows the squad to see what actions should take place on the objective in detail.
- Write the distance and direction to the objective on a piece of paper and lay it in the terrain model, so that everyone knows how far and on what azimuth they will be traveling.

- If you have time (which you probably won't), you can make your model 3D by using the map to determine where hills and creeks will be.

Confirm with Higher

Before briefing your OPORD, *always* confirm the distance and direction with Higher (i.e., higher authority; in this case, Higher is your TAC). This will save you a lot of headaches in case your recorders miscalculated something. There is no excuse for not knowing which direction you should be headed or how far you can expect to travel. Checking your distance and direction keeps you from getting lost and not completing your mission.

Special Teams

As a general rule, no matter what your mission is supposed to be, you need to appoint four different specialized teams: Enemy Prisoners

Pulling security

Pulling security

of War (EPW), Aid and Litter (A&L, first-aid administrators), Demolition (Demo), and Civilians On the Battlefield (COB).

Having all of these teams ready will ensure you are prepared for almost anything that can come your way. It is far better to have an extra team or two and not use it than to need, say, a COB team and not have one.

Slow, Smooth, Fast

In much of what you will do in the Army, you should remember this common mantra: slow is smooth, smooth is fast, so slow is fast. This may seem contradictory at first, but the more you apply it, the more sense it will make.

Consider the briefing of an OPORD. Being nervous and anxious leads to rapid, unclear articulation, misunderstandings, pauses while you try to remember information, and a plethora of "uh's" and "um's." Instead remain calm. The sense of calmness will reflect onto your squad, and a slow, smooth reading will lead to a faster briefing overall, because there will be fewer pauses and fewer questions at the end.

The same rule applies to marksmanship. Rather than firing rapidly and wildly, you'd do well to line up the sights and take the shot consciously. After all, it's not who fires the most bullets who wins, but rather the one who hits the most targets.

Command and Signal

One good thing to add when briefing the Command and Signal paragraph of the OPORD is hand signals. Hand signals *are* signals, after all, and reviewing them in the fifth paragraph is a way to make sure there is no confusion about them. Simply go through about seven of them—and have your squad do it with you, to ensure they understand.

Spot-Check

As part of the OPORD you will do backbriefs (quizzing others, with questions such as "What's our mission?" or "Which team is the

Evacuating a friendly casualty

assault element?") at the end to ensure that all cadets understand the mission that you just gave them. However, don't limit the check on learning to just a couple of questions at that time. Throughout your rehearsals, as you do your walk-through, ask spot-checking questions to make sure everyone is actively engaged and knows what to do during the mission. Example: "All right, Stevens, once we are on the objective, what will Bravo-team be doing?"

Stay Concealed

Throughout the mission, make use of any cover or concealment around you. If your squad halts on its way to the objective, move to the nearest tree or rock and get behind it, rather than just plopping down in the open. When crossing an LDA, the people pulling security should be as far off the road or trail as possible while maintaining a clear view down the linear area. If there's nothing else available where you're stopped, get behind your ruck.

The FRAGO

You will eventually perform a mission in which the TAC will call you after you have begun moving to the objective and inform you that you have a new mission. You will then need to inform your team leaders of your new plan and carry on as quickly as possible.

Usually only a small variation is required. The key to looking good is to issue your FRAGO (fragmentary order) in the five-paragraph format, just as you would an OPORD. A FRAGO is just a modified OPORD, so treat it as such. If there is no change for one or more of the paragraphs (such as command and signal) say "no change."

In addition, it would be wise to have a hand signal SOP for when a FRAGO is being relayed by Higher. This lets your subordinates know exactly what is going on so they can prepare to receive the new mission.

Pulling security

En-route Rally Points (ERPs)

As you are headed to the objective, you should set ERPs for your squad. These are areas to which the squad can withdraw if something unexpected happens. Most people will say "set an ERP every 100 meters," but that can be foolish. Rather than go for specific distances, the person in charge of designating the RPs should instead look for areas that meet the following criteria:

- Be easy to find
- Be off the natural lines of drift (where the enemy is likely to walk, such as trails)
- Have cover and concealment
- Be defendable for short periods

These same criteria apply to objective rally points (ORPs). Make sure they are not in an open area, and that there is plenty of room for

Conducting EPW search

your squad to spread out in 360-degree security, so if someone should throw a grenade in the middle it won't wipe out the whole squad.

3D Criteria

When you spot the enemy, pass the information up using 3D criteria: description, distance, and direction. For example, suppose you are on the leader's recon and you spot the enemy before the squad leader does. In order to let him/her know where the enemy is, you might say something like, "There are three enemies wearing black tops and ACU bottoms and carrying rifles at our 1 o'clock at about 75 meters."

Violence of Action

When attacking, always maintain a high level of violence of action. Run all-out to get to cover and assault the enemy; walking, being quiet, and not having your weapon ready to fire are marks of a poorly trained cadet. You should be hitting the objective so hard that the opposing force (OPFOR) has little, if any, time to react. By remaining on the offensive—hard—you keep momentum in your favor.

Reports

Before you send up a radio report, have all the information prepared ahead of time. Don't call Higher and then take over a minute to give a report because you're saying it as it comes to you. For example, if you're going to send a size, activity, location, uniform, time, and equipment (SALUTE) report, have all the elements written down so you can read them off quickly.

Chapter 8

Patrolling

Many cadets do not get to practice patrolling before they attend Leadership Development and Assessment Course (LDAC). This can cause a great deal of anxiety. However, they should know that a patrolling lane is very similar to a Situational Training Exercise (STX) lane. The difference is that a patrol consists of two squads rather than just one. To adjust, simply treat the squads as if they were merely large teams in a STX lane. Instead of Alfa-team in the front and Bravo-team in the back, it will be first squad in the front and second squad in the back.

Another key difference is that the legs (how far you have to walk from the starting point to reach the objective) of a patrolling lane are often up to five times longer than those of a STX lane. The increased walking, coupled with carrying a much heavier ruck, can be exhausting, so training up before LDAC by doing ruck runs is highly advised.

In addition, the patrol leader (PL) and assistant patrol leader (APL) use real radios during patrolling missions because there are more people to manage, and the patrol will often be very spread out.

Knowing how to effectively use the communication equipment can be very beneficial. (See Appendix G.)

Finally, the planning phase is much longer because you have to break the information down twice: from the company (Higher) to the patrol (the two squads combined), and then from the patrol to the squad's teams. In order to get all the planning done, as well as all of the rehearsals, you must be efficient with your allotted time.

During the mission, the cadre will evaluate not just one cadet (the squad leader, or SL) as in STX missions, but four cadets: the PL, the APL, and the two SLs. Each will receive a rating of excellent (E), satisfactory (S), or needs improvement (N).

Before doing patrolling missions, it would be wise to review the tips given for STX missions (see previous chapter).

Timeline

This is just as important during patrolling lanes as it is in STX, if not more so. You need to have a preset plan for how you intend to disseminate all information and conduct all rehearsals in a timely fashion. Without a good plan for planning, you will look as if your actual planning is haphazard. It is worth your while to sit down ahead of time and figure out a specific, preliminary timeline that should allow you to accomplish everything you need to before stepping off.

Patrol Leader

The PL is in charge of the overall plan. He or she leads from the front, while the APL is in the back. The PL should have his radio telephone operator (RTO) with him at all times. Communication between the PL, APL, and RTO is absolutely key in handling the larger formation. However, the PL should know how to give the SLs room to lead as well.

Assistant Patrol Leader

The APL is in charge of security and accountability. The APL needs to know the PL's job and plan, because the APL is next in line should the PL become dead, injured, or missing.

The APL should inform the SLs of what the APL is doing in case the APL is killed or has to fill in for the PL. The APL knows how to enforce standards and the PL's requirements, while giving room to the SLs to lead as well. The APL helps the PL with collecting reports from the special teams, and sends all reports to the RTO.

The APL should monitor security always, but especially so as to address the most likely and most dangerous avenues of approach. Be loud about security on the objective. In general, the APL watches the PL's rear—both literally, regarding security, and figuratively.

APL and SLs

Many people will say it is too difficult to get an E as the APL or SL, because they simply don't have enough responsibility. It is true that the PL will be the center of attention, but the APL and SL can also make a significant impact. Some ideas:

- Check the camouflage of the squad members. Ensure that their face paint is still on and reflects the guidelines in the unit standard operating procedures (SOPs). Make sure that they smear the paint over their hands, as unpainted hands can stand out. Lastly, have them put foliage—sticks, grass, leaves—on their helmets to break the outline of the dome, so they blend in better with their surroundings.
- Make contingency plans while in the assembly area (AA) and objective rally point (ORP). These are similar to the plans for the patrol base. They should address which direction the squad/patrol would exit from and how far they would go. You will likely need to do a map recon to figure this out.
- Check the subordinates' sectors of fire when they are in the AA and ORP. This ensures proper maintenance of security.

- Make sure squads keep their knee pads up over their knees at all times.

Radio Telephone Operator

The RTO knows radio language, and is dependable and organized. The RTO also should be physically strong—one of the strongest ruckers—due to carrying the big, heavy radios. The RTO collects reports (SALUTE, ACE; see Glossary), informs the PL, and sends them to Higher on behalf of the PL. This allows the PL to focus on the situation.

Check on Your Subordinates

While marching, leadership should be moving back and forth making sure all subordinates are doing well, have no severe foot pain, and are staying hydrated. When they see you're doing the extra movement to take care of them, they'll appreciate it.

Rucks and Rucking

As mentioned, the lanes for patrolling are much longer than STX lanes. In addition, rather than carrying around an assault pack you will have a large, heavy ruck on your back.

For this reason, building leg and lower back strength before LDAC is very important, in addition to actually doing ruck marches while still at your school. Consider doing squats with your ruck on at PT, as well as plyometric exercises.

Even if you are well conditioned, the rucks will be heavy and difficult to carry. When the patrol pauses and you must drop to a knee, don't hesitate to loosen one strap and swing the ruck off your back and to the front of you to use as cover. But, however tempting it may be, do not just sit down and use the ruck as a backrest. It looks lazy, and it's not tactical.

Chapter 9

Leadership Development and Assessment Course (LDAC)

The following tips will help you to excel at camp in general, and especially to be one of the most effective and efficient leaders.

BRING the following

Warm clothes: gator skin, watch cap, etc.
A small pillow
A battery shaver, rather than razors
Mouthwash, to use instead of brushing your teeth while in the field—it's 100 times more convenient
Baby powder
Bandaids, hand sanitizer, and antibiotic
Extras of the Army physical fitness uniform (APFU), hangers, and socks
Laundry soap (powdered, not liquid), but only enough for about 3 loads—you won't need more
Permanent marker, and an alcohol pen and eraser

Some thumb tacks
Small, high-powered, red-lens flashlight
A civilian backpack
Scissors and a knife
Your own binoculars
100 mph tape
Ranger beads
A book, iPod, and/or a deck of cards

Females

Black bobby pins
Black hair ties

DO the following

- Label all of your equipment with your name
- Have several people (friends, family) write letters to you—it raises your spirits big-time
- Volunteer for tasks often—even if they don't sound like much fun
- Try hard at everything
- Keep your cool, even though sometimes you'll get frustrated, whether from lack of sleep or other reasons
- Prepare yourself and others for future days' training
- Learn the name of everyone in your squad on day 1
- Know team-building games to play to meet people and kill time
- Pick the bottom bunk
- Always lock your locker
- Keep bandaids, hand sanitizer, scissors, knife, and antibiotic cream in your Army camouflage uniform (ACU) pockets
- Use the drawstrings on your uniform at all times
- Use your red-lens flashlight for night land navigation and in the tents

Work out days 1 to 3 to stay in shape for the day 5 Army physical fitness test (APFT)—but don't push yourself too hard: aim for about 50 push-ups and sit-ups

When at the tactical training base (TTB) or in the assembly area (AA), pee before going to bed—no matter what

Dummy-cord your canteens and flashlight to your load-bearing vest (LBV)

Put stuff that you want to waterproof (paper, notes) in the Meals, Ready to Eat (MRE) "hot beverage" bags—they're tougher than zip-loc baggies

Use ranger beads to keep track of your pace count

Wear your civilian backpack when doing follow-on training, such as Cadet Troop Leader Training (CTLT)

Use your book, iPod, and/or a deck of cards to kill time during the first and last days of camp

When not in a leadership position

Be a good follower: when told to do something, just do it—even if you think you have a better way

When in a leadership position

Develop plans that fix people's problems/complaints, rather than just smoothing them over

Tell subordinates your expectations

Speak LOUDLY

Wake up at least 15 minutes early to be prepared for the day and set an example

Use the alcohol pen and eraser to write your garrison operations orders (OPORDs) on the side of a locker, so everyone can see them and copy them down (see Appendix B)

Use thumb tacks to post stuff on cork board

After making up squad standard operating procedures (SOPs), post them on the board in garrison

Always recon: know exactly where you're going to go—even while in garrison (see Chapter 4)

Use team leaders when you are a squad leader

Appoint cafeteria runners to let the platoon leader (PL) know when he/she can head the platoon over to the cafeteria

Have squad members label their canteens with tape

Make sure canteens and Camelbaks are filled the night before training

Put nails in your terrain model kit (TMK) to use to wrap yarn around, or as a prop when making a 3D terrain model for Field Leadership Reaction Course (FLRC) (see Chapter 6)

DON'T DO the following

DON'T chew gum while in formation—and definitely not when addressing a cadre member

DON'T point out things other cadets do wrong when Tactics Officers (TACs) are around

DON'T lose your temper; and if you do, don't let it show

DON'T complain—EVER. When others do so, try hard not to join in, even though it will be tempting

DON'T be apathetic. Hold people to a high standard. You can acknowledge that something is dumb (without complaining, of course), but don't be apathetic

Chapter 10

Life as a Cadet

Here are a few pointers that will make life as a cadet smoother as you function on campus:

- Never be later than five minutes early for anything. That means that if you are supposed to be there at 0900, you should arrive no later than (NLT) 0855. (See Appendix F concerning military time.)
- Men should buy their own hair clippers. They should not go more than two school days without shaving their faces.
- If you're in a relationship, be sure to get your other half involved in what you do. Keep him/her informed, and answer any questions he/she may have. Military life is very different from civilian life, and many things you may not think twice about could make no sense to others. (For instance, see Appendices E, F, I, and M.)
- You will find that Reserve Officer Training Corps (ROTC) will take up a big chunk of your time, so don't jump into too many other things right off the bat. Adding clubs and fraternities on top of ROTC may be more than you can rapidly adjust to. Do

not let your grades slip because you're over-involved in extracurricular activities. (Remember Chapter 1.)

- However, you should join at least one non-ROTC organization. It will expand your friend base and give you a break from military life.
- Learn the value of naps! Take them as often as you need to. A good two-hour nap every afternoon can do wonders for a busy student/cadet.
- Get to know the names of everybody in the ROTC program. Start with those in your class, and then work through the other classes. Just knowing who people are can make things much simpler for you.
- Always go through your chain of command. This ensures everyone is in the loop, and that the people in charge are not dealing with every minute problem. Be sure to ask your peers questions before going to the cadre.
- Don't be wasteful. This is good advice for things in general, but place special emphasis on how you use government (military) property. By wasting electricity, gas, bullets, batteries, or anything else, you are throwing away taxpayer dollars. The money that is wasted there is money that could be better utilized, whether to conduct research to improve the existing equipment of combat units or to provide medical care for the wounded.
- Always have a pen and paper handy. When in uniform, carry a notebook in your pocket; when on campus, have one in your backpack. When an idea comes to you, a peer shares information, or a cadre member mentions something—write it down. Do not rely on your memory to recall what was said.
- When in charge of something, be sure to spot-check with your subordinates after issuing the plan. Example: When you are an MS300, check on the MS100s before a road march to ensure they have the correct packing list.
- In general, when in charge, be more laid back with your peers: do not overemphasize that you're the boss. Make it a team effort. However, with subordinates, make sure, through bearing and deed, that they always know you're in charge.

Chapter 11

Leadership Philosophy

These elements are drawn from more-complete leadership philosophies. They come from various sources, including books, cadre, and other military personnel. (For further inspiration, consider reading some of the books listed in Appendix L.)

- *A leader's integrity must be unimpeachable.* A leader's word is his bond. Always pick the hard right over the easy wrong.
- *Leaders set a professional example.* A leader's appearance, candor, and understanding of the Army Values are key to maintaining a professional image. Do not let emotions overcome your professionalism.
- *Leaders are physically and mentally fit.* Being fit makes it easier to conduct daily tasks to a high standard. In addition, by being strong physically and mentally, you are leading by example, because you should want all of your soldiers to have these qualities. Work out no fewer than three days a week, and continue to educate yourself throughout your career.

- *Leaders are technically and tactically proficient.* Leaders should know the profession of arms. In order to lead by example, you must first be an expert in your specialty. This applies to all facets of life, whether you are a teacher, police officer, or Soldier. If you do not know how to do something, ask someone who does know.
- *Leaders communicate.* When new information is made available, leaders share it with everyone it relates to. If unsure about what something means or how to do something, always check with the person in charge as soon as the issue arises. Never dump a lot of new information on people the day of events if it can be prevented, and never wait to ask important questions on the day of an event if you can answer those questions yourself or ask them sooner.
- *Leaders lead from the front.* Leaders should try the hardest, work the longest, get the dirtiest, be the coldest, and LEAD by example! Leadership by example is the highest form of leadership. It is better to inspire subordinates to do what is right than to use rank or position to make them do something. Do not ask your subordinates to do something you are unwilling to do yourself.
- *Leaders are standard-bearers.* Leaders find the standard, meet the standard, exceed the standard, and *enforce* the standard in everything. They set the bar for others around them. If you do not meet the standard, you cannot reasonably expect your subordinates to, either. When your subordinates are not meeting the standard, enforce it in order to maintain the good order and discipline of the unit.
- *Leaders train to standard.* Leaders ensure that all events are properly planned and resourced, so that quality training is conducted. Train to the standard, not to time.
- *Leaders don't waste time.* Wasting the time of subordinates is a cardinal sin. Don't force your subordinates to sit around and do nothing; always have a back-up plan. If there is down time, conduct concurrent training between events. If quality training is complete and the standard is met, let your soldiers leave.

- *Leaders develop.* Leaders develop leaders. Take the time to listen to, talk to, and mentor your subordinates. When another leader is struggling, help him or her out.
- *Leaders prepare subordinates to assume their duties and responsibilities*. This cross-training ensures that information is properly passed on. By doing this you are upholding the standard for future leaders.
- *Leaders expect subordinates to make honest mistakes, and allow for a learning curve*. In every organization, people make mistakes. Leaders do not ridicule or belittle those to whom this happens. Instead, leadership involves allowing people to make these mistakes, then ensuring that they learn from them. Rather than simply stating what a subordinate did wrong, help him/her by discussing the right way to do the task.
- *Leaders counsel.* Leaders let subordinates know where they stand. They are honest and open; they aren't afraid to tell someone they are not meeting the standard. Leaders owe it to the leaders-in-training behind them to tell them how to improve. You aren't paid to "sugar-coat" things; not everyone deserves a trophy. You need to have the intestinal fortitude to look a man or woman in the eye and say, "You're just not cutting it, but here's how to improve."
- *Leaders shouldn't be afraid to trust and take risks*. A leader must be willing to take a risk to develop his/her subordinates; sometimes a leap of faith will pay great dividends in the long run. Being innovative and willing to try something new is a trait that can greatly benefit your unit.
- *Leaders take ownership.* A leader must take ownership of whatever organization he is a part of. By taking ownership and responsibility, a leader becomes a member of a team. Individual responsibility for whatever the unit does, or fails to do, is the role of a leader. You have to care about what you are doing and demonstrate that through example. Apathetic people make poor leaders.

- *Leaders aren't afraid to let subordinates shine*. If the unit does well, leaders place the credit on the unit and/or individuals. If it does poorly, leaders take the blame on their shoulders.
- *Leaders recognize positive performance.* Recognition and praise help with the development of a team. Remember, though: praise good work in public, but criticize only in private.
- *Leaders seek balance in their lives.* Spending time with family or away from the Army will ensure that you as a leader do not "burn out" or get over-stressed from working too much.

Part Two:

How To Improve the Battalion

Chapter 12

Things We Do at Truman

The focus now shifts to ensuring that your battalion is operating at an optimal level. But what follows is just ideas and suggestions. In some cases your school may already be doing these things. In any case, you may want to implement some of these ideas but not others. You may think of other innovative ways to improve upon these ideas. If nothing else, these possibilities may spark interest in trying to make your program stronger.

The Cadet Lounge

This is a room set aside specifically for Reserve Officer Training Corps (ROTC) cadets to hang out together. It's an area where they can relax, socialize, read, and/or do homework. It's a safe haven on campus. Not all schools have a cadet lounge; if your school doesn't, perhaps you could petition to get one. For those that do, here's what's in ours. This list may suggest something your cadre might add:

- Two gaming systems (an X-Box 360 and an Nintendo Game Cube) and a large, flat-screen TV

- Cadet mailboxes (one for each cadet)
- Four computers, with internet connections and a printer
- A white board and two cork boards
- A couch, a love seat, several cushioned chairs, and a coffee table
- A large desk
- A bookshelf containing military history and warfare books
- A subscription to *Army Times*, so we can stay informed on what is currently happening in the Army

Hallway Boards

In our hallways, we have multiple cork boards on which to post all sorts of information. This increases communication among cadets, and informs other students on campus about what we do. The boards contain:

- Photos of all senior ROTC cadets, with their job titles. Examples: physical training (PT) instructors, Cadet Battalion Commander, etc.
- All newspaper articles, official pictures, and letters written to us from people about our program. Example: thanking us for helping with their events
- Photos of all cadets involved in varsity sports/club teams/ intramural sports doing what they do
- Battalion information, including training information. Examples: packing lists, lab locations, contact sheets, and information about upcoming events
- A large world map containing pins that show where cadets have done official Army training. Examples: Basic Training in Oklahoma, Cadet Troop Leadership Training (CTLT) in Germany, Leadership Development and Assessment Course (LDAC) in Washington
- Information on the Army physical fitness test (APFT), including sections that list which cadets got 300+, 290-299, 280-289, and 270-279. It also has photos of the Ranger

Challenge team and information about the competition, including how we placed in each event
- Information on safety, discussing its importance, as well as all the risk management information for the battalion
- National Guard information, including information on what National Guard cadets do, photos of all new National Guard cadets, and for each a map of his/her state with a paper pinned showing where he/she drills, what his branch is, etc.

In addition, general Army recruiting posters are framed and hanging in the hallways, and a brochure and pamphlet stand offers recruiting information for students on campus to look over.

The Classroom

This is where each military science (MS) class is taught. Some current features:

- An Army theme, with sandbags filled with shredded paper and camouflage netting lining the walls
- A display case containing relics from past wars, including old uniforms and various artifacts
- A large sand table with terrain model kit (TMK), used to practice briefing missions
- Two pieces of workout equipment, enabling dips, leg raises, and pull-ups
- A climbing rope attached to the ceiling
- A bookshelf holding field manuals
- A board showing the battalion organization: every cadet's name is on a laminated piece of paper, with a magnet glued to the back; these can be moved around based on who is in charge, allowing people to know who is in what squad, who the platoon leaders (PLs) are, etc.

Our classroom is changing into a "smart classroom" that allows us to record lectures given by cadre members and view them online. This enables students to take the class while studying abroad, for instance.

Field Leadership Reaction Course (FLRC)

Outdoors we have a few obstacles set up that can serve dual purposes: they're workout equipment, and they allow us to practice FLRC lanes. The obstacles include:

- The weaver
- The Rat Hole
- The minefield
- The early warning device
- Low belly over
- The Gorge of Doom
- The Bridge of No Return
- The Overhang
- The secret device
- Downed Pilot

Rappel Tower and One-Rope Bridge

Our rappel tower has separate sides for:

- Regular rappelling
- Practicing the skid (going down without a wall beneath your feet)
- Wall climbing

We also have four posts set up so that two teams can practice doing the one-rope bridge for Ranger Challenge at the same time.

Competitions

Our program allows cadets to compete in various competitions, including the German Armed Forces Badge for Military Proficiency, the Bataan Death March, the Ranger Challenge, and the Ranger Buddy Challenge.

Combat Lifesaver (CLS) Certification

Each school year we do a CLS course, which serves two main purposes: 1) It prepares cadets to handle medical emergencies by showing them how to stop bleeding or make a splint, for example, and 2) It is a great preparation course before LDAC to get cadets familiar with first aid, which is something all cadets are tested on while at camp.

Battalion Newsletter

One senior cadet puts together a monthly newsletter that is a compilation of short articles submitted by other cadets. Their subjects and content range from the Cadet Battalion Commander's brief on the battalion; to various schools, such as airborne and air assault; Ranger Challenge; and fitness articles, like those from which snippets were included earlier in this guide.

Color Guard

Our color guard is made up of volunteers from the freshman, sophomore, and junior classes. Its members practice drill and ceremony weekly.

The color guard participates in ceremonies and special occasions, such as ROTC appreciation night at sporting events and the singing/playing of the national anthem at football games. Also at football games, when our team scores, color guard members fire the cannon and do push-ups equal to the points on the scoreboard.

Rewards and Recognition

Our cadre recognizes cadets who do well at training events and reward them in front of battalion formations. These rewards include an Army combat uniform (ACU)-patterned pocket knife with "Bulldog Battalion" on the blade, and baseball caps with "TSU ROTC" sewn on. The knife, for example, is rarely handed out, and much prized.

Color Guard members fire a cannon after a touchdown

Fundraising

Our battalion has tried multiple fundraising ideas:

- Raffling tickets off to the crowd at football games to fire the cannon after halftime
- Working as ushers, taking tickets at the football games
- Selling fleece jackets with gold Army lettering sewn on them to battalion members to wear over their uniforms at non-training events
- Organizing and conducting a 5k race
- Selling discount cards that entitle purchasers to discounts at various local stores

Community Service

We try to give back to the community by doing various service projects. We have taken part in Toys for Tots, in which the cadets donate toys to the community for Christmas. We have also helped at the local YMCA on Halloween, and gone trick-or-treating for canned goods to stock local food banks.

Fitness Challenge

We have coordinated with our campus student recreation center to do a fitness challenge event each semester. We set up a table and put up a large poster advertising the challenge: seeing how many push-ups and sit-ups the students can do in a minute, and how fast they can do a shuttle run that we set up outside. We give each participant an ROTC shirt, and offer upgraded prizes to the top male and female achievers in each event.

Squad Competition

Sometimes we have squads compete against each other at PT. This could be a race, who can do the most repetitions, or who can complete the most stations. The winning squad gets to give the losing squads a punishment at the end of PT. They might have to sing the Army song, play air guitar to a hit song from the 80's, or perform some goofy movement. This sort of shared experience builds a sense of esprit de corps, and helps make PT more fun.

Garrison Training

In order to give the cadets some idea of what garrison life will be like when they are at field training exercises (FTXs) and LDAC, we try to set them up in as many leadership positions as possible at school. Each week the 100s (freshmen) and 200s (sophomores) have one (or more) class leader who attends the training meeting. His/their responsibility is to pass the information on to their classmates so that everyone knows, for example, where PT and lab will be held.

Similarly, each week the 300s (juniors) have a PL and platoon sergeant (PSG). In addition, the PL and PSG plan a workout for the battalion (synonymous with platoon, at our school) each Wednesday. They receive a blue card evaluating them on their leadership at PT. In addition, they turn in a yellow card at the end of the week covering everything they did while in that leadership position.

Our organization includes four squads. They are set up at the beginning of each semester, and do not change for the entire semester. The squad leader (SL) for each squad is a 300, and they also do not change position, unless they are assigned to be PL or PSG for the week. When forming up the platoon, the SLs take accountability of their squad, and report this to the PSG, just as they will at camp.

Labs

Our unit began doing just one 2-hour lab each week for everyone except the 100s. This saves time for the cadre and simplifies the planning process. For example, when we do situational training exercises (STX lanes), we have four different missions being conducted at the same time, each by a different squad. Though the squads are on the small side (as noted, we have four, instead of two as in years past), this allows more opportunity for cadets to serve in leadership positions.

Mentoring

Each 400 is assigned 3 to 4 underclassmen, from all years, to mentor. The cadets they mentor are called their protégés. The 400s must meet with their protégés at least once a month to discuss SMART goals (those that are specific, measurable, attainable, realistic, and time-limited), Army physical fitness test (APFT) scores, grades in academic courses, and any personal or professional issues/questions/comments they may have.

Weekly Labs

We hold a weekly ROTC lab on Thursday afternoons during which we conduct hands-on training that prepares cadets for LDAC. The training subjects might include STX lanes, issuing operations orders (OPORDs), handling enemy prisoners of war (EPWs), etc.

Nutrition Journals

Cadets who are overweight must keep a journal of what they eat. This helps them better monitor what they are consuming and cut back on calories.

Additional PT

Cadets who do not reach the pre-determined scores for each event on the APFT (example: 80 points in each event, for the 300s) must attend additional PT. This is held at the campus recreation center on Tuesday and Thursday. A 400 leads them through a workout.

Branch Orientation Day

We hold this event, which is mainly a recruiting tool, on the rugby field. We have helicopters fly in, Hummers pull up, medical trailers on display, various weapons laid out, and rappelling demonstrations at the tower.

Working with Sports Teams

We link up with various teams to help them do fun team-building projects, such as rappelling off the tower and going through our FLRC course. We recently provided a physical, boot camp-type training for the women's softball team. Our color guard also presents the flag during the National Anthem at some games.

Swearing-In

We try to make swearing-in a bonding moment, as well as a positive public exposure for ROTC, which can help with recruiting. For example, we have held ceremonies at the local Armory, and at halftime on the 50-yard line at football games.

Organizations

Our cadets founded and take part in several organizations:

- For cadets specifically, there is the RECONDO club, which allows cadets to take charge of, plan, and execute missions. It helps prepare them for LDAC. (See a sample constitution and bylaws for such a club in Appendix A.)
- There is the Sharp Shooter club, which meets to practice firing fundamentals and familiarize members with various weapons. Members compete in an annual rifle competition.
- Much like the various majors on campus, we also have a professional fraternity, which is geared toward the military.

Creative PT

Each month a senior cadet leads a creative PT for the battalion. This helps increase the variety of workouts, gives the junior cadets ideas to use and inspires them to be more innovative, and keeps workouts fun and interesting for prospective students who are thinking about contracting.

Music at PT

Music is strongly encouraged during PT. It makes time go by faster, provides motivation, and distracts cadets from the pain of the workout.

Filming the APFT

At each APFT, we film the junior cadets to ensure that they are using proper technique. This allows them to analyze themselves, so they can identify their own weaknesses and strengthen those aspects before they head to camp.

Color-Coded Boots

Cadets usually have two pairs of boots, and they need to break in both pairs. We have the cadets mark the inside of their boots with permanent marker, one pair in red, the other black. Then we issue directives such as "For the next month, cadets are to only wear their black boots," or "For the ruck march this Friday cadets are to wear their red boots." SLs then check the boots before the event to ensure that everyone is in the proper uniform.

Duty Squad Rotation

Each week the squads rotate so that one squad per week is in charge of maintaining the cadet lounge. They are to make sure papers are stacked, books are not lying around, trash is picked up, etc.

ROTC Orientation

At the beginning of each semester we have all new cadets, and any other cadets who are interested, come to an ROTC Orientation Briefing. It is led by the Professor of Military Science (PMS) and covers a wide range of topics. Some examples:

- Program expectations (including what it takes to keep the scholarship)
- What ROTC clubs there are
- How seriously alcohol-related instances are dealt with
- How the Order of Merit List (OML) works (specifically, how important grades are; see Chapter 1).

Battalion Facebook Page

We have made a page on Facebook on which cadets can post photos from military-related events, ranging from competitions to color guard. We also post news articles related to the Army and a variety of other information.

STX Video

As a class, the 400s have made a video on how to conduct a STX mission. We filmed each step, including receiving the mission, briefing the warning order (WARNO), executing the "take-charge minute," rehearsing the special teams, briefing the OPORD, conducting rehearsals, doing PCIs, and finally movement and actions on the objective. It is organized in chapters, so that the MS300 instructor can show specific chapters in class to give the underclassmen a visual understanding of how things should look.

Designated Driver Phone

We have a phone (donated to us by Wal-Mart) that is used when anybody needs a ride at night. Everyone in the battalion has the phone number. A designated driver monitors the phone, and provides safe rides as necessary.

Chapter 13

Improving Our Battalion

My own program could still be improved upon. Here are some things it could try. Not all can be implemented immediately, but they are goals to work toward. Consider implementing them in your program.

Regarding classroom aspects, military and academic

- To provide underclassmen with help on their courses, post a list of all the seniors and their majors so that underclassmen can go to them for advice.
- To promote the strength and integrity of the academic program, stop giving an A to almost every student in Military Science (MS) classes, because this does not reflect that some did much better than others, nor does it support the higher standards expected of future officers.
- To ensure that cadets are reading their assignments in MS class and taking the time to understand them, administer regular quizzes to check on learning.

- To improve MS class attendance, require cadets with unexcused absences to go to an additional physical training (PT) session.
- To force cadets to think through how they lead, as well as to improve their public speaking skills, use MS class to review scenarios, then have each person deliver a three-minute brief on how he/she would apply his/her leadership philosophy in each set of circumstances.

Regarding military/training aspects

- To improve uniform compliance so that all cadets wear the same, correct uniform, put greater emphasis on enforcing the standard. (Despite reminders through email and at training meetings, some of our cadets still do not wear the uniform as it is described in our battalion cadet handbook.)
- For situational training exercises (STX lanes), recruit social and service fraternities to serve as opposing forces (OPFOR, or "bad guys").
- To enhance cadet understanding of STX through the discussion of after-action reports (AARs) and to improve retention, have lab tactics officers (TACs) do backbriefs afterwards.
- To add variety, compete in Sniper Challenge: it provides a change of pace from regular competitions, and its focus contrasts with other competitions' training for combined multiple tasks that we don't otherwise use.

Regarding PT and health and wellness

- On the Risk Management board (see Chapter 12), include a health and wellness section that displays reminders such as "wash your hands," and offers brochures and pamphlets on good nutrition and exercise.
- To improve long-term fitness planning, draw up monthly PT plans. Any good fitness instructor will tell you that this would be an improvement over haphazardly throwing workouts

together week by week. A monthly plan allows you to more easily measure progress, do periodization, and ensure variety.

- To better reflect current research, stop stretching before workouts, because it leads to poorer workouts, and may increase the chance of injury (see Chapter 2). Instead, simply warming up thoroughly should adequately prepare us for workouts, and the change will save about five minutes that can be devoted to actual physical training.
- To improve our PT warm-up, change it to reflect what science suggests and what elite athletes do; just jogging 400 meters is not enough.
- To better prepare for the 2-mile run (usually the battalion's weakest event), increase the distance of sprints during our sprint days (Wednesdays). Being able to sprint 30 meters hard will not be of much help on the 2-mile run; instead we should run longer intervals (200 to 800m).
- To improve training and PT, construct more Field Leadership Reaction Course (FLRC)/workout obstacles for cadet use.
- Have cadets with unexcused absences from regular PT go to an additional PT session.

Regarding morale/motivation

- For team building, have the cadet Special Projects Officer (SPO) put together events/games such as Capture the Flag or Frisbee on the quad on a Friday night and/or play a game of Assassins a couple of times per semester.
- To build unit cohesion, enhance connections between upperclassmen and underclassmen, thereby encouraging alumni donations to the program in the future, and just have fun, conduct an annual "silly competition" with teams of mentors and their protégés going up against other mentors with their protégés (see Chapter 12). Or have contracted members from each class compete, so that teams of 100s, 200s, 300s, 400s, and cadre have a friendly competition against each other. Award a trophy.

- To commend those who have done well and broadcast their achievements to the school, maintain an awards board. Include the winners of the RECONDO tab, and list all the awards and their recipients from the spring and fall ceremonies (see Chapter 12).
- So that students can see the wide array of places where they could live as an officer, provide a large map of the world and insert colorful pins where program alumni are currently stationed. Put just one pin for each state/country where at least one officer is; to the side of the board list all those places; and next to each place list each officer's name and the year he or she was commissioned from the school. Example: Ft. Bragg, NC: CPT Joe Smith 2007, 2LT Ashley Jones 2010, etc.

Regarding campus/community/potential recruit relations

- For community service, team up with a service fraternity.
- To better integrate with the rest of the campus, allow people outside of ROTC to play in the morale games mentioned earlier as well.
- To help spread the word about ROTC—possibly leading to the recruitment of new cadets by giving them an inside look at what we do—persuade social and service fraternities to volunteer to be opposing forces (OPFOR, or "bad guys") for our STX lanes; they could count the effort toward their service hours. Consider giving each volunteer some kind of ROTC merchandise, such as a T-shirt, as a thank-you.
- To get people who are unfamiliar with our program interested in it and excited about the possibilities, produce a short promo film for each of our organizations, using video clips backed by upbeat, motivational music, and post them on our website and YouTube.

Regarding general improvement

- To get ideas for your battalion, your Cadet Battalion Commander should travel to a different university each semester, tour that battalion's facilities, and meet with its cadre and cadets about their programs.

- To provide feedback, have cadets take twice-a-semester anonymous surveys about their battalion. Each survey should consist of no more than about 10 questions, and there should be provision for written responses. Example questions: "On a scale from 1 to 10, how prepared do you feel for STX lanes?" Or, "What aspect of training do you feel needs more emphasis?"
- To spur critical thinking and conversation about topics that could have significant impacts on the military, have the monthly newsletter poll cadets anonymously on various topics. Example question: "Should women be allowed to serve in the infantry?"
- To help put into perspective what our cadets are doing well and what they should work on, put up a board in the hallway that breaks down the national Order of Merit List (OML), posts the OML list for each class of cadets, and shows national averages for grade point average (GPA) and the Army Physical Fitness Test (APFT), etc.

Appendix A

RECONDO Constitution

RECONDO Club
Constitution and By-Laws

Article I: Name of Organization

A. RECONDOs

Article II: Purpose of the Organization

A. Mission: To further educate cadets about the military, enhance their skills and leadership, and make them more effective in practical applications. In short, the club strives to better these cadets as future officers, and to strengthen their relationships within the organization through service to the community, education, skills enhancement, and leadership opportunities.

B. Goals

- Raise the standard of military education
- Encourage and foster the essential qualities of good and efficient officers
- Promote fellowship among cadets

C. Objectives

- Conduct in-depth courses on military tactics (once a week)
- Conduct situational training exercises (STXs) (five times per semester)
- Enforce military conduct codes and uphold the standards of the Army
- Conduct bonding activities

Article III: Membership of the Organization

A. Eligibility for Membership

1. Members must be enrolled as full-time students at Truman State University. Members must be enrolled in military science or have an in-depth military background/understanding. Members must have a strong dedication to the club, be involved in club events, and be in good physical condition. If more individuals apply to be members than can be accepted, a selection process shall examine involvement in military science, physical condition (APFT score, or abilities in particular events), and/or a paper written by each individual explaining why he/she wants to be included. Being contracted is highly encouraged, but not required. Age, school credits, and ability to pay dues are not considered. Only members who are ROTC cadets are allowed to hold office or have voting privileges.
2. A faculty member/ROTC cadre may not serve as the primary contact person for the organization.

B. Categories of Membership

1. To earn a shirt one must be a member and have a record of attendance at a minimum of 80% of all activities agreed upon by the club for one semester. One must also pass each quiz, with a minimum score of 80%. Each semester every member must take part in either a fundraising or a service event.

2. To earn a beret one must have a record of attendance at a minimum of 80% of designated activities for two semesters, and participate in the RECONDO FTX.
3. To earn a tab one must complete the following:
   A) Achieve a score of at least 80% on the quizzes administered throughout the semester at meetings. Five quizzes shall be given; competitors may fail up to two, but must retake each and pass with a minimum of 80%.
   B) Score at least a 290 on no fewer than two APFTs in a single semester.
   C) Have an overall GPA no lower than 2.75.
   D) Lead at least one lesson that is no less than one hour in length.
   E) Put together at least one OPORD for a club lab that takes place off campus, and must critique the squad leader for that lab.
   F) Lead a squad for a club lab.
   G) Participate in the RECONDO FTX.

All of the requirements to earn the tab must be completed in a single semester. A candidate may attempt it every semester, if necessary. Once earned, retaining the tab requires maintaining a GPA no lower than 2.75, scoring a minimum of 290 on at least 2 APFTs each semester, and receiving no lower than a B in Military Science class.

C. Withdrawal or Removal of Members

- Withdrawal is informal, and is left up to the members' discretion. Attrition is expected due to the physical and mental stress such an organization causes.
- Removal is up to the commander's (president's) discretion, but shall not be carried out without the input of the second and third in command. Grounds for removal include but are not limited to poor attendance and lack of cooperation.
- If there is an issue between members, they are to bring it up the chain of command for resolution.

- If necessary, the appeals process consists of setting up a meeting with a cadre member to discuss the issues in question. If the cadre member believes there was any wrong-doing, a meeting with the whole club shall be held to discuss it. If the club cannot adequately justify the removal of a member to the cadre member, that person shall be reinstated.

D. To Remain a Member

Requirements to remain a member: All members must be involved and committed to the society. This includes maintaining an attendance record of no worse than 80%. Individuals may fall short of the attendance requirement up to two semesters and still remain a member, but these two semesters may not be consecutive.

E. Quizzes

The commander shall administer five quizzes each semester. They are to cover a range of topics pertinent to developing a more knowledgeable soldier, such as first aid, battle drills, and geography. Each quiz shall consist of no fewer than 10 questions. The level of difficulty should be consistent. Questions should cover only material addressed at meetings or in assigned readings. Each quiz shall be designed similar to the following: 1/3 covering previously quizzed material; 2/3 covering material addressed since the previous quiz. All members may retake the quizzes as many times as they need to get the 80%, but those attempting to earn a tab get only two retakes.

Article IV: Designation of Officers

A. Selection of Officers: The Commander shall be appointed each semester by the Professor of Military Science. All other officers shall be appointed to their positions by the Commander, based on leadership qualities and past involvement.

Article V: Officers

A. Description of Officers

1. Commander: In charge of entire organization, oversees all administrative aspects. Delegates work to others, oversees the completion of assigned tasks. Organizes and presides over meetings. Is the chief organizer of the Spring RECONDO FTX. Must have a RECONDO tab.
2. XO: Ensures the tasks assigned by the commander are carried out. Ensures that members know when they are to lead a squad, create and turn in an OPORD, etc. Is in charge of detail work for the FTX. Serves as president when the commander is not able to perform his/her duties. Must have a RECONDO tab. Must have at least a 90% attendance at meetings.
3. 1SG: Records the minutes of each meeting and keeps them on file. Takes the roll and keeps attendance records. Is in charge of social gatherings. Performs any other tasks assigned by either the commander or XO. Must be a 200, with at least one semester of experience.

B. Non-Truman students shall not serve as officers in the RECONDO club.

C. Procedures for Filling Vacated Offices:
   1. All positions shall be filled by appointment of the commander, using volunteers first, then filling in as needed.

D. Procedures for Removal of Officers
   1. Any complaint shall be brought up the chain of command, and shall be dealt with on an individual basis.

Chairmen

A. Urban Land Navigation—Puts together the course for the club's use.

B. Clothing—Orders shirts, tabs, and/or berets as needed. Keeps track of who earns what, as well as expected costs and estimated time of arrival of orders.

C. National Guard Liaison—Preferably a member of the National Guard. Helps coordinate events that involve Guard personnel, such as friendly competitions with and educational sessions by Guard members.

D. Skill competition—Organizes competition that relies more heavily on skill than physical strength (1st aid, calling in a 9-line, checking EPW, firing a weapon, land navigation, paper quiz over FM 7-8, weapon assembly/disassembly, grenade throwing, etc.).
E. Philanthropy—In charge of selecting one service event each semester, such as Big Event, for club members to participate in.
F. Fundraising—Finds a realistic way to raise club funds, such as by selling arm bands, and carries out the effort.
G. Treasurer—Keeps track of all money already in the club account, makes deposits, sets a club budget, and keeps track of who has paid dues.

Article VI: Meetings

A. Company Meetings: To be held once a month, to discuss business. Each member must be present or provide an excuse for absence.
B. General Meetings: To be held once a week, at the discretion of the cadets.
C. Special Events: Optional activities such as camping trips, paintball games, shooting events, parties, cookouts, watching military movies, etc.
D. Service Events: Performance of service around the community.
E. Voting: All members who meet the membership and attendance requirements may vote. A simple majority is needed to pass any measure, unless otherwise stated.

Article VII: Finances

A. Dues/Membership fees
    a. Membership Dues: Dues shall be discussed before the beginning of each semester, and therefore the amount may vary. Dues shall not exceed $60 during any given semester, unless approved by a 3/4 majority.

   b. One member shall be appointed Treasurer at the beginning of each semester, and shall take charge of dues monies paid.

B. Expenditures
   a. All proposed expenditures shall be laid before the membership for discussion, but final decisions shall be made by the Commander, as advised by the XO and 1SG.

C. Dissolution of Funds
   a. If the club or treasury is dissolved, funds shall be turned over to the military science department.

Article VIII: Advisor

A. Selection/Duties
   a. The advisor shall be the Professor of Military Science for the school year.

B. Duties of Advisor
   a. The advisor shall secure materials that the members cannot acquire by themselves.
   b. The advisor shall help get cadre to evaluate STX lanes.

Article IX: Amendments

A. Proposal of Amendments
   a. Proposals may be offered at the beginning of any meeting, either verbally or in writing, by anyone.

B. Provisions
   a. To hold a vote on any amendment, 2/3 of members must be present. All members with an 80% attendance record during the current semester may vote.
   b. Newly passed amendments take effect immediately.

C. Ratification
   a. This constitution and by-laws go into effect immediately.

Appendix B

OPORD for Patrolling

Attack-Patrolling Lane, Truman State University, 151730April2010

Situation	
A. Enemy	Elements from the Caquetá Army's 81ST Rifle Regiment (RR) have been decimated in recent offensive operations. Several senior leaders of the 81st RR have been killed or captured in recent weeks, dealing a devastating blow to their campaign in Palomas. In order to regain the initiative, the 81st RR has been attacking Paloman supply points to disrupt friendly operations. Teams are known to travel in 2-4 men carrying newly acquired small arms and explosives. The 2-4 man teams are known to operate out of temporary outposts. Their current morale is low, but is increasing with each successful attack on supply centers. They will most likely flee if not killed.
B. Friendly Forces	(1) Higher Unit: 10th Bulldog BN conducts attack operations NLT 011730April2010 vic. AO Kirksville in order to destroy enemy outposts and prevent the enemy from attacking supply points. (2) Right unit Mission: Alpha Company, ambushes along AXIS Gray to eliminate enemy reinforcements in OBJ Jamaica in order to prevent enemy link up operations. (3) Left Unit Mission: Charlie Company, recons along AXIS Violet to clear the route of possible IED's.
C. Attachments Detachment	None

Mission	Bravo Company conducts attack operations NLT 011710April2010 to destroy enemy outposts located in AO Omaha vic. WE 32734774 in order to prevent enemy attacks on supply points.
Execution A. Concept	Bravo Company will infiltrate into AO Kirksville with each patrol moving along a separate route to their operations sites.
(1) Maneuver	(1) (Your) Patrol, 1st Patrol is the main effort, will cross the LD vic. WE 32824792 at (H+45) along route orange to mount an attack on enemy outposts located in OBJ Omaha vic. WE 32734774 NLT 011710April2010, 2nd Patrol isolates the OBJ by securing avenues of approach to the OBJ in support of the main effort, 3rd Patrol is in reserve and provides rear security.
(2) Fires	(2) Fires: Company mortar platoon is on call to support 1st patrol's mission. 1st patrol has priority of fire. Request targets through the company's forward observer.
B. Task to Man. Units	1st Patrol, you are the main effort, you will cross the LD (H+45), and move along route orange to mount your attack enemy outposts located in OBJ Omaha vic. WE 32734774 NLT 011710April2010. 2nd Patrol will cross the LD (H+45), and follow the main effort Axis of advance; establish blocking positions to secure avenues of approach and on order be prepared to take on the mission of the Main Effort. 3rd Patrol will provide rear security and remain prepared to provide follow on support to the main effort if requested.
C. Coord/Inst.	(1) PIR: Enemy direction of travel, Communications equipment, weapons, condition of supply, intelligence documents. (2) Reports: Crossing LD, enemy contact, Captured EPWs, ACE after consolidation, and SITREPS as needed.
Service Support	a. General. Company trains located at the CO AA Vic. WE 32824792. b. Material and Services. (1) Supply: Re-supply available at the OBJ following the attack. (2) Class I cycle is: M-M-M.

Service Support, Continued	Top off water in your current positions before moving out. (4) Transport: None (5) Services: None (6) Medical: Casualty collection points at all AA and OBJs. MEDEVAC available upon request. (7) Personnel: EPW collection points located on OBJ
Command & Signal	A. Command (1) Higher Unit Location: Bravo Company CP located at CO AA vic. WE 32824792. (2) Commander is located at Company CP. (3) Succession of Command: CO, XO, 1SG, 1PL, 2PL, 3PL. B. Signal (1) Call Signs: CO=B16, XO=B13, 1SG=B17, FO=B15, 1PL=T17, 2PL=T27, 3PL=T37. (2) Number Combination: 5 (3) Challenge and Password: Blinker/Fluid (4)Running Password: Lightning Time is now_______, What are Your Questions.

	Tactical Evaluation	
EVENT	—Attack Operations	—Frago Mission
TASK:	—OPORD delivered clearly —Rehearsals —Movement to OBJ	—Effectively dealing with civilians on the battle-field. —Safeguarding civilians —Eliminating enemy threat —Reports
OPFOR TASKS	* Civilian tasks: —Make contact with Americans, but make it known that their presence will interfere	* Enemy tasks: —About 1-2 minutes after contact is made between the squad and civilians, open fire.

OPFOR TASKS Continued	with your mission —Explain situation to Americans (see below) —Refuse to leave area	—Should the squad attack, die in place. —Should the squad flee, give chase 100 meters.

Civilian REQUIREMENTS: 2 reporters, ID cards, maps, news report document on possible treaty between Paloman and Caquetá forces.

Enemy REQUIREMENTS 3 soldiers, small arms, documents, OPORDS

SP GRID	WE23824792	MAGNE/A	206 degrees
OBJ GRID	WE32734774	DISTANCE:	200 meters
FRAGO mission:	Upon request for LD		There are reports of American civilian reporters in your AO trying to broker peace between Paloman and Caquetá forces. The mission is to make contact with the reporters and extract them from the area. You must ensure their survival until extraction. *Civilian mission*: You are in the area to broker peace to the Caquetá forces since their war has caused massive civilian deaths. You are refusing to leave the area and any contact you have with American soldiers is seen as a hit on your credibility you have with the Caquetá forces. You can talk with American soldiers, but you must try to limit your contact in order to maintain you credibility.

Appendix C

Sample Physical Training (PT) Plans

Tabata Training

A coach from Japan created a workout that is very brief yet produces great results: Tabata training.

The idea is simple: choose a workout, and try to do as many repetitions in the allotted time as possible. The intervals are as follows: 20 seconds of all-out effort, followed by 10 seconds of rest. Repeat this sequence eight times. Total workout time: 4 minutes.

When the coach used this method on already highly trained individuals, Dr. Tabata noted that in just six weeks of testing there was a 28% increase in anaerobic capacity in his subjects, along with a 14% increase in their ability to consume oxygen (V02max). He concluded that just 4 minutes of Tabata interval training did more to boost aerobic and anaerobic capacity than an hour of endurance exercise. The fact that it worked on athletes who were already in great shape is important, as such significant gains are usually seen only in beginners.

This method works so well because you are able to keep pushing your muscles for long periods with minimal rest, instead of simply doing four straight minutes of an exercise. The key is to never rest during the 20-second bursts. If you need to drop to your knees during push-ups, do so. The exertion should be so exhausting that you are unable to talk during the 10-second breaks.

How can this workout apply to ROTC? Consider doing the four-minute workout in the Tabata format concentrating on various muscle groups. Try, say, 4 minutes of push-ups, sit-ups, squats, and one other exercise for a total of 16 minutes. For the rest of PT, go for a run.

The AK Standard

One problem with group workouts is that people are at different levels of fitness. Therefore, typical ways of conducting PT—calling for either a certain number of repetitions ("Everyone knock out 20 push-ups") or exercise for a certain period ("We'll start with one minute of push-ups")—require too many or too few repetitions for almost every person. Plus, when using the time limit, many people will do a few reps, then go into the resting position to kill time.

To combat these issues, I started something during our Ranger Challenge season that became known as the "AK Standard." (My nickname is AK.) An exercise leader is chosen from among the most fit. He or she designates a type of exercise, then commences performing it. Everyone performs the exercise until the leader stops. The lead person may not go into the resting position, and should not stop until he/she cannot do any more repetitions without rest.

This accomplishes a few things. The person in charge is leading by example, doing the most reps without resting. Others learn that performing the exercise for that length of time is possible. It takes care of the time problem, because if the lead person isn't resting at all, nobody else should be either; individuals may not be doing as many reps as the leader, but they should never stop exerting themselves. And it takes care of the repetitions issue, because nobody is locked into a certain number—they simply do as many as they can before the leader stops.

Various PT Plans

These are all plans that MS300s have put together in the past:

Execution

- Concept of Operations:
  Phase I: First formation, accountability, warm up/movement to track.
  Phase II: Execution of exercises. Squads will fall into designated areas. Area one is the south straightaway; various sprint workouts. Area two is under the east goal post; various upper body exercises. Areas three and four will be under the west goal post; two squads will conduct thumb wrestling, then exercises determined by a win or loss.
  Phase III: Final formation, cool down, announcements.
  Tasks to Subordinate Units: Squad leaders will take charge of their squads and lead them to the track, as well as through the various exercises.

Execution

- Concept of Operations: PT consists of 4 stations. The first station will be Baldwin Hall; a course throughout the building, with a series of obstacles for cadets to negotiate. The second station will be located in the classroom; an upper body workout. The third station will be located by the elevator in the basement; an abs workout. The fourth station will be in the basement hallway; a cardio workout.
  Tasks to Subordinate Units:
  1st squad will start on the obstacle course section
  2nd squad will start on the upper body section
  3rd squad will start on the abs section
  4th squad will start on the cardio/plyometrics section

Execution

- Concept of Operations:
  Battalion will fall in to formation with four equal squads, with A and B teams, NLT 0600.

PL Caldwell will lead Battalion in PT warm-up.
PSG Dilday will introduce PT stations and explain exercises.
Stations:
Push-ups
Sit-ups
Relay race
Jogging
Sprinting
30/60
Planks

- Coordinating Instructions:
  PL Caldwell will move with 3rd Squad A Team
  PSG Dilday will move with 1st Squad A Team
  Each team will start at a different station
  Two teams will start at the relay race station
  Teams will rotate in descending order (1st Sq to 2nd Sq; A Team to B Team) every five minutes
  Squads will fall in NLT H+50 for cool-down led by PSG Dilday

Other Plans Used in the Past

Set up several points across campus, with a list of exercises at each point. Break down each of the four squads into two teams, so that eight units total participate. The teams race through the points to see who can get the most points done before time is up. The losing teams must do a punishment that is designated by the winning team.

Or, with the same eight teams, give each team a Frisbee. Starting PT at a single location, have the teams race each other to the far corner of campus. Each team throws its Frisbee as far as it can. Wherever it lands, the unit must do a certain number of push-ups or sit-ups. It then launches the Frisbee as far as it can again, and continues to completion.

Appendix D

List of Exercises

This list is by no means comprehensive, but it does offer a variety of minimal-equipment exercises that cadets can use and/or modify for their workouts.

- Upper Body
  - Regular push-ups
  - Wide-arm push-ups
  - Close-arm push-ups
  - Diamond push-ups
  - Earthquake push-ups
  - Clapping push-ups
  - Decline push-ups (legs on partner or chair)
  - Pike push-ups
  - Partner-assisted shoulder press
- Core
  - Sit-ups
  - Crunches
  - Front plank
  - Side planks
  - Supermans
  - Diagonal crunches
  - Reverse crunches
  - Holyfields

  Supine bicycle
  Quadruped
- Lower Body
  - Squats
  - Lunges
  - Split jumps
  - Bounding
  - Bunny hops
  - Skipping for height
  - Skipping for distance
  - Knee tucks
  - Ankle bounds
  - Jumping rope
  - Running hills

Appendix E

The Military Alphabet

When using radios, it can be hard to distinguish between sounds and letters. The military therefore uses a special alphabet. For example, when saying somebody's call sign on a radio, instead of pronouncing O21 as "Oh twenty-one," you would say "Oscar two one." For radio usage purposes, it would be wise to memorize this alphabet early.

A: Alfa
B: Bravo
C: Charlie
D: Delta
E: Echo
F: Foxtrot
G: Golf
H: Hotel
I: India
J: Juliet
K: Kilo
L: Lima
M: Mike
N: November
O: Oscar
P: Papa
Q: Quebec
R: Romeo
S: Sierra
T: Tango
U: Uniform
V: Victor
W: Whiskey
X: X-Ray
Y: Yankee
Z: Zulu

Appendix F

Military and Civilian Time

The military uses a 24-hour clock, as opposed to the 12-hour one civilians generally use. This helps clarify timing and eliminates the use of "AM" and "PM" modifiers. To help adjust to saying military time, consider switching all digital clocks to 24h mode rather than 12h mode. The following is a list of all times in civilian format, followed by military format.

12:00 AM—0000 hrs (Midnight)
1:00 AM—0100 hrs
2:00 AM—0200 hrs
3:00 AM—0300 hrs
4:00 AM—0400 hrs
5:00 AM—0500 hrs
6:00 AM—0600 hrs
7:00 AM—0700 hrs
8:00 AM—0800 hrs
9:00 AM—0900 hrs
10:00 AM—1000 hrs
11:00 AM—1100 hrs

12:00 PM—1200 hrs (Noon)
1:00 PM—1300 hrs
2:00 PM—1400 hrs
3:00 PM—1500 hrs
4:00 PM—1600 hrs
5:00 PM—1700 hrs
6:00 PM—1800 hrs
7:00 PM—1900 hrs
8:00 PM—2000 hrs
9:00 PM—2100 hrs
10:00 PM—2200 hrs
11:00 PM—2300 hrs

Appendix G

Radio Phraseology

Knowing key words that are often used on the radio in the military is an important skill. Here are some, with their meanings:

Affirmative—Yes.
Negative—No.
Over—I have finished talking and I am listening for your reply. Short for "Over to you."
Out—I have finished talking to you and do not expect a reply.
Roger—Information received.
Copy—I understand what you just said (after receiving information).
Wilco—Will comply (used after receiving new directions). Implies "roger."
Go ahead or **Send your traffic**—Send your transmission.
Say again—Please repeat your last message (NOTE: ***Repeat*** *is not used, as it is a specific command when calling for artillery fire*).
Break—Signals a pause during a long transmission to open the channel for other transmissions, especially for allowing any potential emergency traffic to get through.
Break-Break—Signals to all listeners on the frequency that the message to follow is priority. Almost always reserved for

emergency traffic or, in NATO forces, an urgent 9-line or FRAGO.

Stand by or **Wait one**—Pause for the next transmission. This usually entails staying off the air until the operator returns after a short wait.

Appendix H

9-Line MEDEVAC Messages

When a soldier is injured, somebody must call for a medical evacuation. The wounded soldier is then carried out of the combat zone by some vehicle, usually a helicopter. Here is the format for the MEDEVAC message, followed by an example.

Line 1 is a coordinate of the pick-up site, to include the grid zone identifier. This tells the MEDEVAC team where to meet you. We use a 6-digit coordinate in most cases, because it provides accuracy down to 100 meters, which should be sufficient for the MEDEVAC vehicle to visually acquire the pick-up site once within range.

Line 2 is the radio frequency, call sign, and suffix of the requesting unit. In short, this specifies how the MEDEVAC team can talk to the requesting unit in subsequent exchanges once the MEDEVAC request has been submitted. This is done because the radio net used to make the MEDEVAC requests is used by everyone requesting a MEDEVAC, so it is reserved for initial calls only. Once a request is submitted, the assigned MEDEVAC team switches to the requesting unit's radio net for any further transmissions needed between them.

Line 3 is the number of patients, listed by precedence. This establishes for the MEDEVAC team the priority of evacuating patients, based on how severe their injuries are, since time of response can determine whether a casualty lives or dies, or loses a limb or eyesight. There are five categories of precedence:

1. Urgent is assigned to emergency cases that should be evacuated as soon as possible and within a maximum of 2 hours in order to save life, limb, or eyesight, to prevent complications of serious illness, or to avoid permanent disability.
2. Urgent-Surgical is assigned to patients who must receive far-forward surgical intervention to save their lives and stabilize them for full evacuation. These patients need to be evacuated within a maximum of 2 hours.
3. Priority is assigned to sick and wounded personnel requiring prompt medical care. This precedence is used when the individual should be evacuated within 4 hours to prevent his/her condition from deteriorating to such a degree that he will become an Urgent case, or whose requirements for special treatment can not be readily fulfilled locally, or who will suffer unnecessary pain or disability by waiting longer.
4. Routine is assigned to sick and wounded personnel requiring evacuation but whose condition is not expected to deteriorate significantly. The sick and wounded in this category should be evacuated within 24 hours.
5. Convenience is assigned to patients for whom evacuation by medical vehicle is a matter of convenience rather than medical necessity.

Line 4 is any special equipment needed by the MEDEVAC team. Special equipment might include a respirator, for lung wounds; extraction equipment, for cases where a proper hard landing zone cannot be established, such as in a jungle; and various types of litters, used for different casualties.

Line 5 is the number of patients, listed by type: litter and ambulatory. Litter patients are those who must remain lying down, usually on a stretcher or litter; ambulatory patients are those who can sit up. This is entirely determined by their wounds. The MEDEVAC team needs to know the distinction between them because it affects how many vehicles must be dispatched, since litter patients can take up more or less room than ambulatory patients, depending on the vehicle. (Litters can be stacked in some vehicles.)

Line 6 is the security of the pickup zone. There are 4 possible statuses:

1. <u>Alfa</u>—No enemy troops in the area.
2. <u>Bravo</u>—Possible enemy troops in the area. No active engagement.
3. <u>Charlie</u>—Enemy in the area, approach with caution. Recent or active engagement with enemy nearby.
4. <u>Delta</u>—Enemy troops in the area, armed escort required. Active engagement near or around the pickup site.

Line 7 is the method of marking the pickup site. Many options are available. Some typical methods:

Chemlights (night time)
Flares (night time)
Smoke or colored smoke (day only)
VS17 panel

NOTE: In some cases, the marking method is not established until the MEDEVAC vehicles are in the area. This prevents the enemy in the area from eavesdropping and potentially using the same marking method to draw the MEDEVAC team into an ambush.

Line 8 is the patient nationality and status. This information is provided in case there are special circumstances for different types of patients, such as a patient being a prisoner of war. The 5 possible combinations of nationality and status:

U.S. military; U.S. civilian; Non-U.S. military; Non-U.S. civilian; Prisoner of war

Line 9 is the level and type of CBRNE contamination. This prepares the MEDEVAC team for entrance into a compromised environment. Usually when helicopters are used not much preparation is done, because the rotor wash tends to blow away any chemical or biological agent. Otherwise, a MEDEVAC typically will not be dispatched if there is any chemical contamination, as any vehicles used in a chemical environment need to be scrapped afterwards.

The following is an example of a full 9-line MEDEVAC message radio exchange:

"Goose, this is Maverick. Over."
"Maverick, this is Goose. Send. Over."
"This is Maverick. Request MEDEVAC. Over."
"Roger, Maverick. Send your request. Over."
"Line One—LZ Robin 87632514. Break."
"Line Two—HF 231.47, UHF-116.4 Maverick. Break."
"Line Three—3A, 2C. Break."
"Line Four—A. Break."
"Line Five—3L, 2A. Break."
"Line Six—P. Break."
"Line Seven—C. Break."
"Line Eight—A. Break."
"Line Nine—All clear. Break."
"How copy my last? Over."
"Roger, Maverick. Solid copy. Stand by for inbound MEDEVAC plan. Over."
"Maverick standing by. Over."

Appendix I

Recommended Books

Grant and Lee: A Study in Personality and Generalship by J.F.C. Fuller

Kill Bin Laden by Dalton Fury

Leadership: The Warrior's Art by Christopher Kolenda

Once an Eagle by Anton Myrer

One Bullet Away by Nathaniel Fick

The Art of War by Sun Tzu

The Killer Angels by Michael Shaara

The Mission, The Men, and Me: Lessons from a Former Delta Force Commander by Pete Blaber

The Unforgiving Minute: A Soldier's Education by Craig Mullaney

Appendix J

Army Ranks

Being able to recognize Army rank can prevent a lot of headaches. Knowing who outranks whom can simplify many tasks and clarify who is in charge of what. Below is a list of ranks. Spend some time memorizing them.

Rank	Rank
 Second Lieutenant, O-1 (2LT) (gold bar)	 Colonel, O-6 (COL)
 First Lieutenant, O-2 (1LT) (silver bar)	 Brigadier General, O-7 (BG)
 Captain, O-3 (CPT)	 Major General, O-8 (MG)
 Major, O-4 (MAJ) (gold leaf)	 Lieutenant General, O-9 (LTG)
 Lieutenant Colonel, O-5 (LTC) (silver leaf)	 General, O-10 (GEN)

Insignia	Rank	Insignia	Rank
	Private, E-1 (PVT) (no insignia)		First Sergeant, E-8 (1SG)
	Private, E-2 (PVT2)		Sergeant Major, E-9 (SGM)
	Private First Class, E-3 (PFC)		Command Sergeant Major, E-9 (CSM)
	Specialist, E-4 (SPC)		Sergeant Major of the Army, E-9
	Corporal, E-4 (CPL)		Warrant Officer, W-1 (WO2)
	Sergeant, E-5 (SGT)		Chief Warrant Officer, W-2 (CW2)
	Staff Sergeant, E-6 (SSG)		Chief Warrant Officer, W-3 (CW3)
	Sergeant First Class, E-7 (SFC)		Chief Warrant Officer, W-4 (CW4)
	Master Sergeant, E-8 (MSG)		Chief Warrant Officer, W-5 (CW5)

Appendix K

Battle Drills Smart Sheets

The following sections cover the main types of mission challenges you will face during Situational Training Exercise (STX) lanes. These step-by-step guides tell you how to conduct the missions. Note that different instructors may teach some variations in how to conduct the missions; these are the methods that worked best for me. Discuss ideas with fellow cadets and cadre members, and don't be afraid to try your own plans. Note: "on signal" refers to a whistle blast.

Ambush Execution

1) Cross LD and call Higher.
2) Set RPs along the way.
3) Conduct a Silent Listening Halt.
4) Set up an ORP.
5) Leave GOTWA with B-team (support) leader.
6) Leader's Recon: left and right security, SL, 2 rear security, A-team (assault) leader, claymore guy.
7) Establish an RP, establish left and right security, set up claymore.
8) Leave GOTWA with rear security at RP.
9) Return to ORP with A-team leader.

10) Put B-team and A-team elements into position, have team leaders camouflage them, and then check everyone. Call Higher.
11) Initiate fire. Primary: Claymore/AT4; Secondary: SAW. Fire for 10 seconds. If there's movement, fire for 10 more seconds.
12) Assault team cross OBJ, separating weapons from the enemy. Support team turns around and pulls security. Spend no more than four minutes on OBJ.
13) EPW team checks bodies and clears dead off the road. A&L tend to wounded.
14) Send SALUTE and ACE reports to Higher.
15) Fire in the hole: 1–A-team leaves; 2–B-team leaves; 3–Demo lights fuse; SL, demo team, left and right security and rear security leave.

If spotted, either break contact through team bounding, or attack and bound forward.

Squad Attack

1) Cross LD and call Higher.
2) Set RPs along the way.
3) Conduct a Silent Listening Halt.
4) Set up an ORP.
5) Leave GOTWA with A-team leader.
6) Leader's Recon: SL, A-team leader, security/observation team.
7) Security team stays at RP, SL and A-team leader return to ORP.
8) Brief plan to team leaders so they can prepare teams.
9) Go through the RP. A-team sets up support, SL sets up assault (L-shaped formation).
10) Call Higher when in position.
11) Use time hack so assault doesn't give away position. Three minutes after setting up, support opens fire.
12) On signal, support shifts fire. Assault moves to last covered/concealed position.
13) On signal, support lifts fire. Assault pops smoke and assaults through to LOA.

14) Support crosses LD to LOA, then teams set up 360 security.
15) Send up ACE and SALUTE reports. EPW and A&L teams do their jobs. Demo gathers enemy equipment if needed.
16) Fire in the hole 1, 2, and 3.

Knock Out Bunker

1) Cross LD and call Higher.
2) Set RPs along the way.
3) Conduct a Silent Listening Halt.
4) Move until under attack. SL call Higher upon contact.
5) Support element (A-team) lays down suppressive fire.
6) Assault element (B-team) flanks the bunker.
7) B-team leader calls in artillery, if available.
8) B-team fires the AT-4, which cues the A-team to shift fire. Simultaneously, bunker team moves to last covered position.
9) On SL signal, A-team lifts fire and bunker team assaults through to LOA.
10) B-team assaults through to LOA. Then A-team assaults through to LOA.
11) Team sets up 360-degree security. Delivers ACE reports. EPW and A&L teams are called in. SL calls Higher with ACE and SALUTE reports.

Area Recon

1) Cross LD and call Higher.
2) Set RPs along the way.
3) Conduct a Silent Listening Halt.
4) Set up an ORP.
5) Leave GOTWA with B-team leader.
6) R&S Team 1, R&S Team 2, and RP team move to RP.
7) Leave RP team at release point with GOTWA, and R&S Teams conduct recon using the fan method. If detected, break contact and move back to ORP through the RP.

8) After recording as much PIR as possible in the allotted time with a Recon log and a sketch, R&S Teams return to RP. Call Higher with SALUTE report.
9) All teams return to ORP and disseminate information. Call Higher for further instructions.

React to Near Ambush (within 30 meters)

1) Team in contact gets down and returns fire.
2) SL assesses the situation. If we attack . . .
3) Team in contact throws grenades and assaults through.
4) Team not in contact lays suppressive fire. Shifts fire, then lifts fire as attacking team nears objective.

React to Far Ambush (more than 30 meters)

1) Team in contact gets down, seeks cover, and returns fire.
2) Team not in contact flanks the enemy and assaults through.

Squad Organization

There are several schools of thought on how to organize your squad. For example, some demand that the team leaders be at the front of their squads, because they should be leading the way. I chose not to do that because I feel the team leader will have better awareness of his/her squad/can see them better if he/she is not on point. In addition, the point man should be worried about running into the enemy or booby traps, not on giving hand and arm signals and making sure everyone is spaced properly. Following is a sample of how I arranged my 11-person squad for various missions.

11 members **Bold=ambush**, *Italics=bunker*, Underlined=recon

A1

A3 A2

A5 A4

SL

B1

B3 B2

B5 B4

A1—Demo, Alt. EPW: **Rear sec**, R&S1 sec

A2—Compass, A&L, Alt. COB, Alt EPW: ***SAW***, RP

A3—TL: R&S2

A4—Pace, A&L, Demo, Alt COB: **Claymore, R sec**, R&S2 sec, RP

A5—RTO, recorder, time keeper, terrain model: RP

SL—R&S1

B1—TL

B2—EPW, Alt Demo, 2nd pace: *Bunker clearing*, R&S2 sec

B3—EPW, Alt Demo, 2nd compass: **AT4, L sec**, *Bunker clearing*, RP

B4—COB, Alt A&L: **Rear sec**, *AT4*

B5—COB, Alt A&L: R&S1 sec

Appendix L

Variable Lanes Smart Sheet

The following variable lane tips were compiled by LTC Reinsch, an instructor with Ranger and Sapper tabs. A variable lane means that you receive a FRAGO during a mission, diverting you from doing a regular drill (knocking out a bunker, conducting an ambush, etc.) to doing something more abstract (linking up with media, talking with a surrendering OPFOR member, etc.).

General Rules for Handling Variables

- Security, Security, Security: Often you will be distracted by the COBs, but you must always remember to keep 360-degree security.
- Control the situation and don't panic.
- You're the SL, make a decision: Don't spend too much time contemplating what to do; just act.
- Once a decision is made, be assertive. Not only will this instill confidence in your squad about your decision, but it will show the COB who is in charge.
- Always maintain one level higher of readiness when dealing with armed individuals. For example, if they have weapons in their hands but hanging by their sides, your weapon should be at the low ready.

- Always use an overwatch element (support) when confronting enemy, non-combatants, etc.
- Use the COB/EPW team to move forward and search and secure before SL goes forward.
- If COBs resist letting you search them, have them conduct a self-search.
- Verify potential allies' identities: ask them, then call Higher to verify.
- If they are allies, have them drop magazines and clear their weapons.
- If the SL is female, be prepared to assert your leadership tactfully; some cultures don't respect females.
- Avoid bringing anyone into your perimeter. If you have to bring someone in, ensure they are searched and under control.
- If the COBs don't speak English, try to use one of your soldiers as a demonstrator. Avoid key words that seem to make them panic.
- If you have to use a translator (say, a cadet on your squad) to communicate with the COB, make sure you talk to the COB directly, not the translator. This shows that your attention remains on the COB.

Appendix M

Acronyms, Abbreviations and Specialized Terms

As you may have noticed, the Army uses a plethora of acronyms, abbreviations and specialized terms, which can be confusing or frustrating. The list below includes key acronyms and abbreviations. Taking some time to memorize their meanings will make you a more confident and knowledgeable cadet. For the sake of clarity and comprehension, it also explains some other terms used in the course of this book.

100s, 200s, 300s, 400s: First-, second-, third-, and fourth-year cadets in an ROTC program

1SG—First Sergeant: The senior enlisted soldier in a company/troop/battery

3D

(1)—Description, Distance, Direction: The information passed up when the enemy is spotted

(2)—three-dimensional

AA—Assembly Area: Where the squad begins its missions

AAR—After Action Review: A tool the Army uses to discuss an immediately past mission and prepare for the future; it consists of reviewing what was supposed to happen, what did happen, and sustains and improves

ACE—Ammo, Casualties, and Equipment: The report you call for after coming under attack or attacking, so that you know how much ammunition your people have left, whether anyone is injured, and whether any equipment was lost or broken

ACU—Army Combat Uniform: Worn to labs, and to class by 300s and 400s

A&L—Aid and Litter: The team that provides first aid to injured soldiers

AO—Area of Operations: Where you are currently conducting missions

APFT—Army Physical Fitness Test: Used to gauge your fitness level; consists of push-ups, sit-ups, and a 2-mile run

APFU—Army Physical Fitness Uniform: Worn to physical training

APL—Assistant Platoon/Patrol Leader

ARTEP—Army Training and Education Program

Cadre—The officers and NCOs who lead instruction

CASEVAC—CASualty EVACuation: Occurs when organic forces (such as your own vehicle) evacuate a casualty

CBRNE—Chemical, Biological, Radiation, Nuclear, Explosives: The dangerous elements a unit may encounter, or be tasked to find

CER—Comprehensive Evaluation Report

CO—Commanding Officer: Officer in charge of the unit

COA—Course Of Action: The plan you intend to implement

COB—Civilian On the Battlefield: Non-military personnel in your AO

COE—Contemporary Operating Environment: Where you are currently operating

Contracting, contracted—Result of a cadet signing a contract obligating him or her to serve a certain number of years in the military in exchange for a scholarship and officer commission, etc.

CTLT—Cadet Troop Leadership Training: A program in which a cadet shadows an active-duty Army officer

CULP—Cultural Understanding and Language Proficiency: A program that allows cadets to experience another culture and possibly practice a foreign language

DA—Department of the Army

ENDEX—END of EXercise: Declared by the evaluator when the training is over after a mission, so that everybody knows they can stop being tactical and prepare for an AAR

EPW—Enemy Prisoner of War: A bad guy you captured

ERP—En-route Rally Point: Places to which your squad or patrol should fall back should they become overwhelmed or lost

FITT—Frequency, Intensity, Time, Type: Principles of exercise planning

FLRC—Field Leadership Reaction Course: A group of scenarios used to evaluate leadership ability

FRAGO—FRAGmentary Order: An amended OPORD

FTX—Field Training eXercise: A larger version of STX; units train in the field for an extended period

GOTWA—Where you are Going; Others going with you; Time you expect to be gone; What to do if the leader doesn't return; Actions to take if the unit comes under attack while the leader is gone/Actions the leader will take if under fire while on recon: A GOTWA is issued any time a person or group leaves the main body, in order to keep everyone informed; most often associated with performing a leader's recon of the objective

GPA—Grade Point Average: number indicating cumulative results of your academic performance

Higher—Higher authority: Example: the Commanding Officer

IAW—In Accordance With: Used to signify the materials used as references

IED—Improvised Explosive Device: A general term for a homemade bomb, often installed on the sides of roads to ambush vehicles

IOT—In Order To: Example: "1st squad will attack the enemy IOT disrupt their activities in our AO"

JFTX—Joint Field Training Exercise: Same as a regular FTX, but done with other units to train on, for example, coordination of logistical matters and tactics

KIA—Killed In Action: Applied to someone who has died in combat

Lane—The specific mission you are to conduct for STX or patrolling. For example, "For this lane you will conduct a movement to contact"

LBV—Load Bearing Vest: Article of clothing that holds your ammo, canteens, compass, etc.

LD—Line of Departure: The point you cross when you step out of the AA to begin your mission

LDA—Linear Danger Area: An open area where the enemy is likely to attack; includes roads and trails

LDAC—Leadership Development and Assessment Course: The camp that all cadets must pass to become officers; it tests cadets' abilities to accomplish multiple tasks

LOA—Limit Of Advance: The farthest you want your teams or squads to go, past the objective, when assaulting it; the LOA prevents them from going much farther than needed

MEDEVAC—MEDical EVACuation: Occurs when outside help (such as a helicopter) evacuates a casualty

METT-TC—Mission, Enemy, Troops, Terrain, Time, Civilians: An inclusive term that encompasses all the major factors a leader should consider when planning a mission

MIA—Missing In Action: Applied to someone lost during a mission

MOPP—Mission Oriented Protective Posture: Basically used to tell you whether you need to have your gas mask on. Different MOPP levels require different layers of gear:

MOPP Level 0—Overgarments, gloves, and overboots are accessible; protective mask remains in carrier at side

MOPP Level 1—Chemical agent detectors are worn; overgarments are worn; mask remains in carrier at side; gloves and overboots are readily accessible

MOPP Level 2—Overgarments and overboots are worn; gloves and mask are readily accessible

MOPP Level 3—Overgarments, overboots, and mask are worn; gloves are kept ready

MOPP Level 4—All protection is worn

MS—Military Science: General title of the academic courses taken by ROTC cadets. Example: MS 101

NCO—noncommissioned officer: an enlisted soldier beyond the private level

NG—National Guard: A state-directed entity that drills one weekend a month and two weeks a year

NLT—No Later Than: The absolute latest time that something must be completed

OAKOC—Observation and fields of fire; Avenues of approach; Key terrain; Obstacles and movement; Cover and concealment: A term similar to METT-TC, except it pertains specifically to the terrain and all the major characteristics you should consider about it

OBJ—Objective: The exact area where you are to conduct your mission, or the mission itself. Example: "Your objective is to knock out that bunker" or "I am going to take a team to get eyes on the objective"

OEF—Operation Enduring Freedom: The mission name for our involvement in many places, but most commonly used for Afghanistan

OIC/NCOIC—Officer In Charge/NonCommissioned Officer In Charge: Those who lead an event

OIF—Operation Iraqi Freedom: The mission name for our involvement in Iraq

OML—Order of Merit List: The ranking of cadets based on scores in various areas of achievement; some, such as GPA, are weighted more than others

OPFOR—OPposing FORces: The "bad guys" you are to gain information from, observe, or attack

OPORD—OPerations ORDer: The five-paragraph order that lets you know the situation, mission, execution plan, services and support expected, and command and signal arrangements

ORP—Objective Rally Point: The last stop before conducting a leader's recon of the objective, and making the attack; you will generally drop your rucks and pull 360-degree security at the ORP

PCI/PCC—Pre-Combat Inspection/Pre-Combat Check: Inspection/checking of troops to ensure they know what they're doing and have appropriate gear

PIR—Priority Intelligence Requirements: The intelligence elements that Higher wants to know more about, and that you will have to find during your mission
PL—Platoon/Patrol Leader: The person in charge of that unit
PMS—Professor of Military Science: The officer in charge of an ROTC program; usually a Lieutenant Colonel or a promotable Major
POW—Prisoner Of War: Applied to someone who has been captured by the enemy
PSG—Platoon Sergeant: The enlisted soldier who assists the PL and focuses on small units, teams, and crews
RECON—RECONnaissance/RECONnoiter: The observation of an area, such as the objective, in order to gain information so as to make an informed decision, before bringing up the whole unit
RECONDO—RECONnaissance commanDO: Title given to a cadet at LDAC who has met all of the established criteria, such as obtaining a certain score on the APFT; the cadet equivalent of an Army Ranger
ROTC—Reserve Officer Training Corps: A program that provides training to cadets that culminates with the cadet becoming an Army officer
RP—Release Point: The area designated by the SL through which the squad passes before setting up an attack
RPE—Rating of Perceived Exertion: The amount of pain one feels while exercising
R&S—Reconnaissance and Surveillance: the team that helps the SL conduct a leader's recon, which then may stay in position to monitor any changes in the enemy situation while the leader returns to the unit to bring it up to the objective
RTO—Radio Telephone Operator: The person in charge of sending and receiving reports via a radioRuck—short for rucksack: The over-sized military backpack used to carry clothing, food, and other amenities
SALUTE report—A report that covers the details about the enemy that Higher may be interested in knowing. The elements: S–Size; A–Activity; L–Location; U–Uniform; T–Time sighted; E–Equipment. Example: S–2 personnel; A–patrolling;

L–EG12345678; U–black shirts with ACU bottoms; T–2130; E–RPG (Rocket-Propelled Grenade launcher) and small arms

SAW—Squad Automatic Weapon: The machine gun a squad or patrol uses during STX/patrolling

SITREP—SITuation REPort: A less formal report. It simply describes what is going on

SL—Squad Leader: The person in charge of that unit

SMP—Simultaneous Membership Program: A program that allows cadets to drill with their National Guard units while also being ROTC cadets

SOP—Standing (or Standard) Operating Procedure: The guidelines established by Higher that determine how your unit will act, dress, etc. Example of usage: "We will be packing our rucks according to the SOP"

STX—Situational Training eXercises: Missions conducted to evaluate cadets on their leadership abilities

Sustains and improves—Given during an AAR to determine what was done well and should be continued, and what needs to be done better for the next mission. Example: Sustain tactical movement. Improve use of hand signals, because not everybody used them

TAC—TACtics Officer; sometimes considered to stand for Train/Teach, Advise/Assist, Counsel: The officer or NCO who evaluates the cadet(s)

Tactical—As in, "being tactical" or "remaining tactical" or some behavior that is "not tactical": Conducting oneself in a professional, military, operational way that makes mission success more likely. Example: Taking cover behind objects rather than pulling security in the open

TLP—Troop Leading Procedure: The eight-step method a leader uses to plan a mission: receive the mission, issue a warning order (WARNO), make a tentative plan, start necessary movement, recon, complete the plan, issue the plan, and supervise

TMK—Terrain Model Kit: The supplies (usually pieces of paper and yarn) used to construct a hasty model of how the mission will unfold from the AA to the OBJ

TTB—Tactical Training Base: Temporary base near combat area from which a unit will often deploy
UAS—Unmanned Aerial System: Used to drop bombs or conduct surveillance
USAR—U.S. Army Reserve: A federally controlled entity that drills one weekend a month and two weeks a year
WARNO—WARNing Order: Basic information provided in advance of the OPORD to prepare troops for what's coming
WIA—Wounded In Action: Applied to someone hurt in combat
XO—eXecutive Officer: The officer second in command. Assists the CO and coordinates supplies

Bibliography

Anderson, O. *The Perfect Warm-up*. Retrieved from http://www.Runnersworld.com/article/0,7120,s6-369-370—11973-0,00.html#

Burfoot, A. *Does Stretching Prevent Injury?* Retrieved from http://www.Runnersworld.com/article/1,7124,s6-241-287—7001.html#

Clark, Nancy. *Sports Nutrition Guidebook.* Champaign, IL: Human Kinetics, 2008.

Howley, E. T., and B. D. Franks, *Fitness Professional's Handbook, 5th Edition.* Champaign, IL: Human Kinetics, 2007.

Jorn, L. *Nutrition*. Kirksville, MO: Truman State University.

Koch, A. *Resistance Training.* Kirksville, MO: Truman State University, 2010.

Nieman, D. C. *Exercise Testing and Prescription*. New York: McGraw-Hill, 2007.

Stamford, B. "High intensity exercise helps burn fat during, after workout." *Army Times*, January 25, 2010.